From Persecution To Praise

My Damascus Road Journey

Cedric Doss

Copyright © 2017 Cedric Doss
All rights reserved.
Photograph by: Amy Deanes
Liberation's Publishing LLC ~ West Point, MS. 39773
All Scriptures quoted from the Authorized King James Version of the Holy Bible
ISBN: 978-0-9891348-5-9

Dedication

I dedicate this work to those among us who have had a tough journey from the cradle to this moment. There IS a blessing in the storm. So, be encouraged, God has not forgotten about you. He has a plan for your life. Giving up is never an option. Hang on in there. Your purpose is to be great in the Lord. God has done His part. It's your move now!.

TABLE OF CONTENT

Introduction 1

Losing My Father 7

Losing My Mother 11

Losing My Brothers 27

Picture Day 37

A New Home 51

My Visitation From Daddy 65

Gaining a Family 73

A House Of Prayer 83

Boys and Girls 95

The Feast of all Feast 103

Another Heart Break 111

Mama J 119

A Taste For Blood 131

Lord Help Us 139

A Call For Help 149

Facing Momma 161

A Downward Spiral 167

Locked up 173

The Voice Of The Lord 179

Prologue 189

ACKNOWLEDGMENTS

"One generation passeth away, and another generation cometh; but earth abideth forever." ~Ecclesiastes 1:4~

I must say it has been exciting, yet bitter-sweet, in getting this book together. But it would have been next to impossible without the passing of one generation—my father. Therefore, I would like to acknowledge him, Bro. L.C. Doss, Sr. Rest in peace, Daddy. Others along the way that played a major role in the birthing of this book were: Bigdaddy and Bigmama Clemons(may you both rest in the arms of Jesus. You taught me what God's love looked like. Thank you!), Almetria Poole-Deanes, Shirley Murdock, William (Annie) Henderson, Inez Haughton, Randy Kelly, Rick Lockridge, Pastor John (Hazel) Smith, Pastor Steven (Sharon) Davis, Pastor Fluid Carr, Jr.; My be-loved children Latelvin, Sierra, and Cedric Jr., My fiancé, K-Rena, for loving, believing and pushing me to make my vision a reality.

Pastor Cedric Doss, Sr..

INTRODUCTION

Life is a journey. From the time we are born until the time we transition, we are traveling. There are hills to climb. There are curves to make. There are rearview mirrors. There are windshields. Then there are other travelers along the way. No one knows what is ahead. Even in the daylight hours when we think we can clearly see our way without the headlights, we do not have a clue to what will happen next. The control we thought we had quickly vanishes when we hit black ice or a puddle of water, and what we are driving veers off the road and lands in the ditch. It is in the ditch where we find a place of unrest and discontentment. We never miss the opportunity that lies before us while looking at what laid behind us.

Sometimes we do not want to accept the idea that a loving God would allow us to go through what we go through on our journey. Does He know it does not feel good when we are traveling on our journey and suddenly have a flat tire or the engine light comes on? Or, in the case of Saul (Paul) knocked from your beast and blinded?

Saul (Paul) was on the road to Damascus as part of his journey. This route had been carefully planned and engineered by God before Saul (Paul) was conceived in his mother's womb—like your route and my route. God is no respecter of persons, therefore, each of our journeys have been prearranged by a God who knows what He has to do to get the best out of us. If it means knocking you or me off of our beasts and blinding us, then that is what He does.

On Saul's (Paul's) journey there were two opposing views being manifested. His will and God's will. Present was an opposition and an opportunity. Paul was on his way to persecute more Christians while God had created an opportunity for glory. What Saul (Paul) did not know was that his opportunity was hidden in his opposition. The opportunity to praise was hidden in the opposition to persecute. Just as mine and yours.

Of course on our journey there are many variables. Variables are those things that can be thrown in at any time upsetting our straightening out the situation. A positive outcome is what we all want. Let me remind you that we cannot control the variables, but to get from persecution to praise, we must control our perspective of the variables. How we see them determines our ability to successfully deal with them. We can either allow them to defeat us or we can see them as an opportunity to go to the next level of our spiritual growth cycle. The choice is ours.

It has been said the journey is as valuable as the destination. It is in the journey that we find change—that we are transformed. Transformation is a unifying language of God's. He cannot use us until we are transformed. Only He has the power to do that. His desire is for all of us to see the light (Light)—to be knocked to the ground from whatever we are riding on that is blinding us to our God-given purpose.

Like Saul (Paul), God did not want me to continue to invest in my own failure—to continue on my journey, in a path, that was leading me to nowhere. Going to persecute the Christians was what lead him to praising God.

Unknowingly, Saul (Paul) was on his way to persecute when God had arranged it for him to praise. He left the house with a mind to harm and ended up meeting the

King! So, I guess it does not matter how our journeys begins, but more about how they end.

Our steps have been ordered by the Lord. Our Damascus roads were not planned along the way as we traveled. No. God is more organized and orderly than that. Our Damascus roads were planned just before God rested on the seventh day.

From Persecution to Praise is my own personal story that led me from a place filled with problems to a place filled with promises—God's promises. I pray that as you read the words in this book that you will find hope as you journey through the life that God has planned for you. Never give up no matter how hard you are knocked to the ground. God has a plan for your life and He has to do whatever is necessary to get your attention.

I will be the first to admit the journey has been more than surprising. Like Saul (Paul), there was no turning back once my appetite for the Lord had been wet. My life was in ruins. Mundane and mediocre living no longer worked for me. Not now and by God's grace and mercy, never again.

Words cannot express the joy I feel that you are taking this journey with me. No trip is joyful when we travel alone. Several years ago this expedition began and I am still on it. Mind you, I have traveled through some wide paths, some narrow paths, some dangerous paths and some exciting paths, but I kept moving. Of course I would like to tell you that the sun has always blazed across my face or the cool winds of ease blew through the downed window and washed me cool, but that would not be totally accurate. To the contrary, there have been some days that I would have to pull to the side of the road because the rain was hitting my windshield so hard I could not see. On many occasions I have had to whisper a prayer to my Lord to give me the strength to defeat the loneliness that had packed bags alongside mine. Yet, I have met many strangers who were on the same road as I traveled and when our eyes met we knew Who we were serving and immediately decided that we were not in a race against one another, but in a race to the end.

So far it has been quite a ride. In the pages of this book, we will travel over spiritual territory that will cross over mountain peaks and cross into valleys deep. The journey is worth it though. Around one bend we will find something to smile about while around another we will find something that puts us on our knees. Either way the reward for taking the journey with Jesus will be well worth it. So buckle your seatbelt, take your lives out of park, past neutral and let us drive into the destiny God promised to those who love Him.

LOSING MY FATHER

"LC!" a voice cried. "Somebody done shot and killed LC!" I was just a toddler when I heard these words. They came from a distance as I walked home from playing up the dusty road from my house. "Who is that?" I thought. "What are they saying?" The closer I got the faint voice became louder and louder. It was the voice of my cousin, and there was no mistaking that or the words she repeatedly screamed. I shook my head in disbelief, but it did not shake away the reality, my daddy was dead. Someone had murdered him.

That night seemed liked the darkest and coldest of my life. I was just a toddler. Relatives and neighbors filled our home. They seemed genuine enough, so at first I tried being strong. I walked around with a stony silence, hardened from anger and disbelief. Those words were the worst words I had ever heard. The weight of it all burdened me. I felt helpless and determined at the same time. It was like carrying too many bags of groceries up a tall stair case with everyone watching but no one offering to help. I almost fell, but I was determined to be strong.

After all the guest had gone it was time for bed. Bedtime was different. As I lay my weary soul down to sleep the weight of it all consumed me. It was when I was all alone that I let the tears stream down. They streamed down heavy and hot like fire burning my cheeks and running into my silent yet screaming mouth. My soul was pained before I ever discovered what a soul was. I wanted my daddy. I wanted to wake up in the morning with his hug. I wanted to watch him leave for work, wait for him to come home. My mom, brothers, and sisters all comforted one another. They even tried to console me. It didn't work. I still felt all alone. My daddy was gone.

The following Sunday my daddy, LC Doss Sr. was laid to rest at the church cemetery in our hometown Prairie, MS. To my family's surprise, as well as mine, the funeral was larger than we imagined. There was standing room only. My little toddler body walked around in amazement at all the faces. There were many family members, neighbors, my daddy's friends and co-workers. They had all come out to celebrate my father's life and pay their last respects to him like he was a hometown hero.

I thought about the man who had killed my father. He was human and deserved to be loved. I couldn't see it at the time, but I later came to realize that no matter who you are, or who your parents are, your life can take on a new path. There are no certainties. You have to take up a new vision. That vision will lead you to a new place where you can be completely reborn, completely new.

Though it made no sense to do so, I would sit and imagine I was a little boy that had gotten separated from his father. I dreamed he was looking for me, and that we would someday be united. That wasn't the case. I wasn't lost, and my father wasn't looking for me. He was dead, gone, transitioned to another world. He would never hug me again, kiss me again. These daydreams consoled me for only a little while.

As time passed, my world took on a whole new look. It went from being safe and secure to being hard and lonely. Lacking compassion, I refused to connect to others, and I refused to allow others to connect with me. I had made up my mind to let the anger consume me. I thought of evil all the time. I came to the realization that once a man's mind was made up to do evil, he did it. Nothing and no one could stop him. Hence the thoughts of my father's killer. He had made up his mind to do an evil thing and carried through with it to my and my brother's and sister's detriment.

Spiritually, I slowly began to lose my way. Without my father leading and guiding me, showing me what a man of God looked like, I grew angry and bitter. Was I becoming like the man who killed my father? God help my soul.

LOSING MY MOTHER

I had a favorite spot when I was little, and I would go there almost every day. It was where I did most of my daydreaming. I had just tied my shoelaces when I overheard my mom talking in the other room. She sounded so upset. Her voice trembled as she spoke. "I just don't think I can do it. With LC gone it's going to be tough. It's too many mouths to feed."

I felt confused. I tried to think really hard about what I'd just heard. My eyebrows squelched together as I took in everything she was saying. I eased closer so I could get a better listen.

"Maybe some of my relatives will take them. If not, the younger ones will have to leave. I'm just not able to take care of all these kids without my husband" I couldn't believe what I was hearing. I turned quickly on my heels and ran out of the house, my worn shoes flapping in the wind and the family dog barking after me.

I kept running. I ran so long and so fast that the tears I cried whipped into my ears. They didn't even have a chance to hit the ground. I kept replaying in my mind what I'd just heard, my head shaking in disbelief. "She can't be referring to me. My mamma can't want to give me away." Something in the pit of my stomach knew better. I was one of the youngest of my mom's seventeen children. There's no way she could be speaking of the older kids. They can take care of themselves.

I kept running. I ran all the way to my spot. No day dreaming today. All I could do was keep replaying in my mind the words, "I can't do it! I can't do it!" How dare she say she can't do it?! How can I, a little five-year old boy be such a burden to anyone? "I never asked for anything." I reasoned. It didn't even bother me that sometimes I had to wear the same pair of clothes twice, sometimes three, times a week, or that my shoes were two sizes too big because they were the only ones left at the yard sale. It didn't bother me that I slept in a bed with three other people. It didn't bother me that I could only have one piece of chicken when I wanted two. It did bother me that I was going to separate from my mother and other siblings. That was too much.

How could my mother choose such a terrible thing? God had taken my father, and I had no say in the matter. It was a done deal, God's choice to remove him from this earth. I was still grieving from the loss of my daddy. How could fate deal me so many deadly blows at once? I thought my mother needed me around to help her with pain. I needed her and I thought she needed me. Who could I turn to now? I felt like a fighter in the boxing ring with no experience. I was being pummeled to death.

I had nowhere to turn. On one side, I had a father who was gone to heaven. Only his memories lingered, but when I reached out for him there was nothing. On the other side, there was my mother I could see and touch her, but there was nothing there to grasp hold of. She had detached herself from me. How can someone be here and gone at the same time?

By the time I reached my spot I was exhausted from grief and despair. My legs gave way and I tripped and fell onto the tall thick grass face first. I was angry. I tried pushing myself up but the dog jumped on my back in an attempt to play. "Stop it! I yelled at him. He didn't listen. He kept trying to play brushing his paws all over me. It only made me angrier. He pressed his face to mine in an attempt to lick my face. "No! Don't do that!" I yelled. I didn't want a dog's love. I wanted my mom. I wanted her to love me enough to keep me.

He wasn't giving up on me. In hind sight I think it was God's way to comfort me. My dog continued to try and play with me. He kept trying to show me how much he loved me, but I rejected every move. I treated him cold, hardheartedly. I knew I needed him around to help me through this pain. I wanted him around, but something inside me was becoming so cold. I was so full of rage now. I took it out on my friend, my pet.

Finally, he got the message and walked away. I knew this was new to him. I had never treated him so poorly. Before, no matter what was going on he was by my side. He had never felt that type of rejection. I was treating him how I felt I was being treated. I thought about that as I jumped to my feet. I called out to him, but he kept walking in the opposite direction with his head hung low and tail between his legs.

"Come back!" I called out and whistled at the same time.

I didn't want my best friend to feel like I felt. It hurt my heart that I had behaved that way towards him. What was I becoming? What did he think of me now? I would not treat him the way my mother was treating me. "Come here boy!" I cried as the compassion rose up in me. He understood. He forgave me. His love for me hadn't left.

I could tell he was careful though. I had made him unsure. There was a rift in the trust of our friendship. Despite this, we walked home together and as we reached the back door of my house I fell beside him hugging him. I ran my hand back and forth along his back. "Sorry boy." I consoled. I was genuinely sorry. I wanted him to know that before I went inside to go to sleep.

The next day I arose to the reality of what I had heard the day before. My mom had packed a few bags and sat them by the front door. A feeling of deep anguish filled my soul. I was terrified. It was as if something had attached itself to me and sucked every bit of life from me. I was weak, and I knew those clothes were mine. I slumped to the floor and cried. She had made up in her mind to give some of us away. All I could do was stare at the bags.

I cried so much my tears had blurred my vision. "Why doesn't my mother want me?" I thought to myself. I wanted to yell but the words stayed stuck in my throat too afraid to pass my lips. "How am I going to make it without my mom and dad?" My sorrow turned to rage. As I shook my head back and forth and paced I decided to confront her for doing this.

I could hear mom in the other room. "Lord I wish I could keep my babies, but I just can't do it without LC!" I became so bitterly angry with my mother. My tiny hands briskly brushed away the tears from my cheeks. I stood tall, walking past my favorite wooden rocking horse I had gotten for Christmas. It meant nothing to me now. Everything I once loved meant nothing now. I walked right up to my mom and confronted her for deciding to destroy my life.

"Why, mama? Why?" I demanded an explanation. She reached out her hand to me and dried my face from tears. I could see the weariness in her face. She looked so drained, "It's for the best Cedric. You will understand better as time goes by." I slapped her hand from my face. How dare she touch me? I didn't want her touching me, not my face, not my hands, nothing. At that moment I hated her.

Just then a knock came from the front door. Immediately my older sister ran to answer it. "It's probably the social worker." My mom said. "It's time Cedric. It's time." I yelled from a place so deep it almost took my breath. "Nooooo!" I screamed. "I don't want to go mamma. I want to stay here with you!"

"It's for your best Cedric. Mamma can't take care of you. You deserve more than I can give you. Go Cedric! Go!"

"But I don't want to go mamma! I love you!" I yelled while falling onto the floor. Why was this happening? A slave had it better. A slave's parents had no choice. They couldn't fight to keep their baby. My momma was giving me away, and there was nothing I could do about it. I hated her at that moment. I hated and loved her at the same time. That kind of madness can damage a child for a long time. I was forever enraged and the fire would only grow more vicious.

"It's okay." I heard an unfamiliar voice say to me. The voice of the man startled me, and I stopped crying long enough to see who it belonged to. In my heart I was hoping it was someone coming to bring an end to all this madness. Obviously it wasn't. The voice sounded white and when I turned to look it was definitely a white man. No white people lived in our neighborhood. So it had to be the social worker my mom was waiting on, he and his coworker Mrs. Jo who was also white. They both stood there emotionless like they had done this thousands of times.

My mother knelt down beside me and my baby brother. She gripped our shoulders and stared blankly into our eyes. She tried to speak but got choked up. It seemed to hurt her, what she was doing, but it wasn't enough to stop her from moving forward. She regained her composure and spoke to us through a deeply pained and hoarse voice.

"You all heard what I had to tell the judge. I have to let you go, because I can't provide a good home for you, not one you deserve. Since your daddy…" She paused. It was as if just the thought of daddy dying took away all the fight in her. She seemed so weak. She closed her eyes to hold back the tears. She opened them after a few moments still blood shot red and swollen from tears. "Since your daddy is gone there's no way I can raise you boys the right way. I don't know how to keep you from the streets. I can't fill your bellies with food, not without money. Giving you up for adoption is the hardest thing I have ever had to do in my entire life, but it's a sacrifice I have to make. I pray one day you will understand."

I couldn't understand. I gazed at my mother with so much anger. With clenched teeth and fist balled tight at my sides I demanded, "How can a mother give away her children?"

"Because it's what's best, Cedric. I've told you.

"You don't love us enough to keep us?" I begged.

"Oh Cedric, don't you understand? It's because I love you so much that I'm able to give you away."

I was silent. I had nothing else to say. I resisted the urge to reach out to her, in spite of a part of me wanting to. If you love someone you want to keep them close. You did not send someone you love away to live with strangers. I refused to understand my mother's mixed up thinking. It was toxic. My entire body ached with confusion and shock.

"When do I have to leave?" I asked with teeth still clenched.

"Now" replied my mother. "The social workers are here to take you all now both you and your brothers.

"Please mamma! No!" my brother LC sobbed. His small face was blotchy from the tears as he quickly latched on to our mother's leg. He refused to let go. I felt like I was dying. My father had died, now my mother. Though she looked alive there had to be death inside of her, a cold emptiness that was placed there with the death of my father.

I desperately grabbed my mom by the neck. "We don't' want to go mamma." I cried.

"Baby it's for the best." She softly responded while gently removing my arms from around her neck. I kept resisting. I forced them back refusing to let go. I had to fight for her, because the moment I wasn't able to hold on I knew it would be the end.

My mother's voice trembled with tears. She had fought so hard to hold them back up until now. She tried to smile through them, but only appeared hollow and drained. She opened her mouth to speak.

"Mr. Loftin and Mrs. Jo promised me that you will all have a clean bed of your own. You'll have good wholesome food, schooling, and clothes. These are all things I can't give you." She paused and looked into LC's eyes. He was still clinging to her leg as I was still clinging to her neck. She then looked at me. She held onto us both as she stood up.

I stared at her hoping she could see inside my soul, see the hurt and loneliness her decision was causing to overtake me. I thought I had gotten through to her, but she only replied, "Don't you see how much it hurts me to see the four of you go?"

"Then keep us mamma please!" I cried out as she began to pull my tight grip from around her neck. I held on for dear life, but she was stronger than I was. I felt like all my strength had gone and my legs were weak, but as she placed me on the floor I gathered the strength to bravely stand on my own two feet.

Mr. Loftin and Mrs. Jo stood impatiently by shifting from one foot to the other. My mother turned to them. LC's grip was loosened from her leg and suddenly we were detached from our mother. The only mother we had ever known was gone, stripped away like soiled clothing. My mind felt stripped, my body, my soul. The only person left to cover me with these things choose not to do so. I was dead; an empty shell of a child the only thing lacking was my tomb.

I don't remember my mother saying anything else after that. Her voice was silent and though her lips parted no words came out of them. Her eyes fell on us as if she wanted to get one last look at the boys she was sending away. She shook her head in dismay before blowing us each a kiss and turning to walk away.

I watched my mother stroll down the hallway, a feeling of dread continually filled my heart. I so desperately fought to control the manic episode that was developing in me. I wanted to run and scream after her, my heart beating out of control, my breath shallow, and hard. For just a second she glanced back at us just before disappearing into the bedroom.

"Nooo!" I screamed falling to my knees. Mr. Loftin lifted me from the floor and tried to stand me on my feet. I had no strength left. My legs defied me and refuse to hold up my pitiful little body. My arms flailed, my feet stomped, I screamed as loud as I could in an attempt to keep them from taking me. It didn't work. Mr. Loftin tired of trying to make me stand and gently picked up my small frame of a body and carried me to the waiting car. He strapped me in the back seat, closed the door, and went back into the house. He then brought out my little brother LC and strapped him in the seat next to me. He was only four years old a year younger than I was. Lastly Mr. Loftin returned to the car along with Mrs. Jo. He carried my one year old brother, and she carried my newborn baby brother.

Before I saw where they placed them I once again began to scream and cry. My eyes were blurry and I couldn't see where they placed the other two. My legs were too short to reach the floor, so I flailed them about wildly. "Let me out of here" I yelled while reaching for the door trying to open it. "I want my mamma!" I cried.

My cries invoked a domino effect, the siblings who had quieted down began crying again first LC, then the one year old, then the new baby. The large sedan was assaulted by our cries. We wanted out. We wanted to be taken back into our home where our mother and our refuge were. It was the only place we had ever felt safe. How could we feel safe with two strangers? Two strangers that looked nothing like us, and cared nothing for us. If they did they would not have taken us from our mother.

My heart felt like it had been stabbed a thousand times. As soon as I heard the engine start I knew there was no going back to our mother. Something inside me knew there was no need to cry any longer. It would not get you back home. Besides I was tired. I was more tired than I'd ever been before. The car moved backwards, then forward clearing its path. I used my tiny elbows to lift up high enough to see through the back window. The place that had once been my home faded farther and farther away in the distance until it was gone.

It was the fall of the year and as night fell a chill came upon me causing goosebumps to rise on my arms. My outside matched my inside now. The car continued to travel up the now dark highway to God knows where. LC, who was sitting next to me, had fallen asleep and his chin rested on my chest. He was slumped over in such a way that made me believe he was getting some of the best sleep of his life. My other two brothers were quiet, and I had no idea if they were sleep or not.

Darkness had fallen over the interior of the car, except for a small beam that streamed from an object I couldn't identify. I could see the outline of our captures. Mr. Loftin was driving and Mrs. Jo was sitting in the front seat next to him. They too sat silently as we all traveled on the smooth paved highway. We hit a pothole. It startled the baby and he made a sound, but went right back to sleep. My stomach flipped flopped as we coasted up and down a hill.

I had no idea where they were taking us, so I sat quietly, anxiously looking out of the window next to me. The tears had dried and I had gotten some rest during the drive. I didn't sleep long, because I wanted to know where we were going. I felt the car began to slow down, and I jerked my head up to look around outside. I used my elbows to push up and get a better look through the windshield. My eyebrows raised in curiosity as I noticed we were pulling into a covered porch that was attached to a red brick building.

"We're here." Mrs. Jo said as if here was as place we wanted to go. I looked at her as she gathered our things in her hand.

"Where are we?" My hoarse fragile voice asked.

"You're in a safe place." She responded as she opened the door.

"LC." I whispered while shaking him from sleep. Slowly he opened his eyes and looked around.

"Where are we?" He whispered back.

I shrugged my shoulders too and replied, "I don't know. The lady said we're in a safe pace."

"A safe place?" he repeated looking around.

"Yes." I replied as I followed his stare.

Just then the back door opened. Mr. Loftin had gotten out of the car and opened the door to help us get out. He reached inside of the car and unbuckled me first, then LC. "Come on young men." He told us both. He was very patient with us as we slowly climbed out of the car onto the pavement.

"Boys welcome!" a woman I had never seen before greeted while kneeling beside LC and me. She corralled us into her outstretched arms. I started to cry again. Once again, I set off a domino effect. LC started crying, then the one year old, and then the newborn.

"They're criers!" the woman said in wonderment while standing up to her feet. She was also strong. She held both my brother and I in her strong arms as she stood. She carried us both through the double glass doors while Mr. Loftin held it open. That would be the last time I would ever see my two youngest bothers. They did not come with us. They remained behind

LOSING MY BROTHERS

As I lay in bed I gazed at a ceiling I couldn't see but knew had to be there. I had no sense of time, but it felt like the darkest part of midnight. The entire room was black, and the only noise came from my little brother's light snoring as he slept alongside me. Everything I knew and loved was gone, and although Mr. Loftin and Mrs. Jo meant well, they had no idea how hard it was for me being without my mom and dad. My entire world had been destroyed. I had no sense of being or belonging anymore. Nothing was definite. Nothing was sure. I floated in a world of limbo unanchored from reality.

This would not be my first time in an unfamiliar place, but this was definitely the beginning of misfortune. It was the beginning of a drastic unfortunate change that happen so fast it did not give my brain time to catch up. "It could all be a dream." I thought. "It could be one of those dreams that have day and night and the next day in them." I reasoned. That was my imagination trying to come back into play. It didn't work. This was no dream, and there was no joy flowing from my spirit. There was only pity. I pitied myself and my little brother. I questioned,

"What can I do to change this?"

"I can think my way out of this." I thought.

"I'm good at that. I… can…" I began to cry. "Think my way … no … no I can't. Not this time Cedric." I reasoned. "The odds are stacked too high against you." In this darkness I cried and cried again. The more I cried the more I longed for what was familiar. I wanted my mom to hug me. I wanted my dad to pick me up. I wanted my bed. "I wanted my home." I cried out loud waking my little brother.

"What's wrong?" LC's tiny voice whispered to me. He had wakened, and I hadn't noticed, so I rolled over to face him.

"What's wrong?" I repeated back to him in the same manner.

"Yes." He asked again. It was as if he had forgotten what we had just gone through.

"I want to go home." I replied through sobs.

"I know. I do too." he painfully agreed.

"What are we going to do?"

"What can kids like us do?

"I guess nothing, since nobody wants us."

"Yeah, I guess nothing."

"I wonder what they did with our brothers"

LC humped his shoulders before replying. "I don't know."

I suddenly became angry again and troubled. "Nobody better not hurt them! If they do I'm go kill'em!"

"Like that man did our daddy." LC blurted out.

I glared at LC through the darkness. His response took me by surprise. Was he implying I was a killer? I was not prepared to answer him. I lay there for what seemed like three minutes staring blankly towards LC before I answered him. The shock of the question soon passed. My brother's concern for me being a killer was not enough to quiet my anger. Nothing did. I thought back to how I had treated my dog. I thought back to how my momma kept moving my hand from around her neck while I tried to hold on to her. I thought back to how I felt walking home the day I heard my cousin yell, "Somebody done shot and killed LC!"

"Yes LC. Yes, just like that man killed our daddy!" Even as a little kid the anger burned in me. It burned like fire, but unlike the Holy Ghost this fire would burn my heart and turn it into stone.

After a while we fell back to sleep. "Good morning." came the cheerful sound of the lady who had picked LC and I up and carried us in the night before. LC had fallen asleep again. I sat there yawning trying to keep my eyes open. "Good morning." I replied while trying to come out of the deep sleep I had fallen into. "Rise and Shine." She said. I said nothing back to her at all. There was nothing to be so cheerful about.

"Did you have a good night's rest?"

"Yes." I said looking over at LC who finally started to slowly move.

"Good morning, LC." She smiled looking at him.

"Good morning." He said softly.

"Where are our brothers?" I demanded. I had fallen to sleep with them on my mind. I had promised myself that I would plant that question in the front of my brain. I was determined not to let another minute go by without asking about them. "They're here in another part of this facility."

She said as she motioned for us to get out of bed.

That wasn't a good enough answer, so I repeated myself again with a hint of intensity. She glared at me through her learned smile. Her eyes spoke to me what her mouth did not say. "Who do you think you're talking to li'l boy." She glared. I wasn't moved. I kept my eyes on her. She huffed at me as if the tone of my voice didn't matter, but the look on my face didn't change. My eyes demanded an answer.

"I don't know who you think you're talking too little boy, but I ain't your momma!" She snapped. "Now, as I said before your baby brothers are doing okay. They're not your worry."

Not my worry, this idiot of a care taker had really struck a nerve with me. Is this how you deal with children that had just suffered so much upheaval? I shrieked back at her bitterly, "They are my worry. They're my brothers and I love them! AND I'm glad you ain't my momma!" How dare she speak about my mother?

I had to hold it together, but those words broke me down. I knew she wasn't my mother. I had to defend myself, and see after my brothers, all three of them. We had no one else. Crying stood for weakness, and I had to learn to suck it up. At five years old that was a hard choice to make. I chose to be strong, but in hindsight I was really hardening my heart. I stayed defensive, ready to pounce and show my toughness to all those around me. Neither my brothers nor I would be treated unkind by anyone without me dealing with it. This was the beginning of sorrows. I would never trust people ever again.

Later that day we were escorted from our room. We had just finished eating lunch, hamburger, fries, chocolate cake, and milk. The caretaker who had so rudely stated she wasn't my momma was carrying our bags. The sight of her sickened me.

"Where are we going now?" I asked as I looked at her and then our bags.

"To a city called, Jackson, Jackson, Mississippi. Have you ever heard of that place?" She asked ignoring my indignant looks. My brother and I were on either side of her as we continued down the long corridor.

"Why are we going to Jackson, Mississippi?" I responded ignoring her placid question, my eyebrows raised in confusion.

"It's what your social workers requested."

"Jackson, Mississippi?" LC asked. "Where is that?"

"It's south of here, towards Mississippi's coast."

"Huh" he replied in confusion.

"It's south of here." She redundantly stated looking down at him as we walked.

"Are we going to meet our mother there?" I wanted to know feeling kind of hopeful.

"No, Cedric." She began. "Your mother has given up all her parental rights. She doesn't want you or your brothers anymore."

"But … Why?" I cried. My weakness came against me and tears began to fill my eyes spilling over my tender face.

She stared at me. "Cedric I don't know why. It's her decision and hers alone. We have to abide by her directions and find a permanent home for you and your brothers."

My hope left. Just the thought of just maybe we would be going to Jackson to meet our mom had made me let down my guard. I realized then hope and hardness did not go together, so I relinquished hope. It was my enemy. My momma didn't want us. She had told us herself, and now a complete stranger was telling us the same thing. "Damn Momma." I thought. She was my weakness. I let the anger return. I would no longer let my love for her break me down again. I secretly reached up to my face and wiped the tears away with the back of my hand, and swore that would be the last time I'd let tears give away my weakness.

We continued to walk in silence as I tried to come to terms with the fact I wasn't wanted. LC wasn't wanted. My baby brothers weren't wanted. It dawned on me my two younger brothers weren't with us.

"What about our little brothers. They're just babies. Aren't they going with us?" I asked.

"No." she responded. "They're not going with you. You will probably never see them again. They are going to a different place."

"But … Where?" I demanded stopping dead in my tracks to look up at her.

"I'm not sure." She shrugged back at me like I'd just asked her what we were having for dinner.

I bit down on my lower lip daring the tear to fall from my eyes. I commanded my emotions. My weakness would not break me this time. I stood strong, my little face hardened like a flint. I would not let a smile escape it. Just then we turned into the office area where Mr. Loftin and Mrs. Jo awaited us.

"Cedric! LC!" They said simultaneously with a smile. I did not return one back to them. Why were they smiling anyway? Was their life all perfect, because mine wasn't? In the midst of it all I ended up next to Mrs. Jo while LC stood next to Mr. Loftin. Someone said. "Are they all packed and ready to go?" I'm not sure who, because everything started to fade away. I think I had a lapse in consciousness, because the next thing I remembered was being once again in the back of the same car that had ripped us away a day ago.

We were headed to Jackson, Mississippi. I had no idea where Jackson, Mississippi was. I was curious though. If curiosity killed the cat, it should have killed me on the spot, because I was more curious about going there than anywhere I'd ever been.

Cedric Doss

Picture Day

The rays from the rising sun coming through the window strewed brightly across my face causing my eyes to pop wide open. I looked all around. I was still sitting in the back seat of the same car behind Mrs. Jo riding shotgun. I glanced over at my brother who was awake but sitting still as a mouse staring straight ahead. I thought he might be looking at Mr. Loftin who was yet again driving, but there was no way he could see him through the gray, crushed-velvet seats. He was out of his view.

We pulled up to yet another adoption facility. How did I know? The same red brick on the outside of this building was on the outside of the building we had just left along with the word Mississippi Home for Children. Besides, I figured, where else would the same two social workers be taking us, if not to another adoption facility?

Once again hot tears rimmed my eyes. Just as Mrs. Jo was opening my door, they flowed down either of my cheeks. I started crying, crying harder this time than I had before. When will this madness end for LC and me? The water kept coming, kept coming, from my young eyes.

"It's okay," Mrs. Jo assured me patting me on my back. Her pats meant nothing to me even though I believed she meant well. I was too emotional to even think twice about her intentions. The blade of the knife was being driven deeper and deeper into my soul and nobody seemed to be noticing the blood flowing except for my little brother, L.C. He was now crying hard and loud. The two of us caused a discorded string of noises anyone who worked in places like this could easily recognize. It was the cry of pain.

Like before, my brother and I were led inside of a well-lit building to an awaiting group of unfamiliar faces. Not only were they unfamiliar, but they were also hard to make out due to the tears coming from my eyes blurring my view.

Inside of Mississippi Home for Children, whose address was State Capitol Street Jackson, Mississippi, was a long bench on which many abandoned children sat shoulder-to-shoulder silently with blank stares. Once I dried my eyes, amongst the unfamiliar faces I noticed; a freckled-faced girl with long red hair to match; a very dark-skinned boy with big eyes and big lips to match; a porcelain-colored girl sitting next to him with short hair and bangs. None of the many children sitting on the long bench appeared to me to be happy. How well did I understand, because I too felt the exact same way.

On a table sitting by the door was a pile of clothes that looked freshly pressed. There were blue trousers and white shirts for the boys and blue jumpers and white blouses for the girls. Just after I noticed them, a man stepped from among the unfamiliar, blurred faces, with some sort of equipment held between his thick white fingers. "Hello," he said gently to all of the children sitting on the bench.

I refused to speak to him. None of the other children did either. We did not want to. Could he not see that we were all hurt and confused and wanted our mothers and fathers? Apparently not, because he scanned us with his blue eyes and proceeded to speak with a smile, "Today we have some good news for all of you." We dropped our heads simultaneously refusing to look up. Good news was taking us back home, and that was not what he was saying.

He went on, "As I was saying, we have some good news for all of you. Would you like to hear what it is?"

He had kept the same gentle tone in his voice as before. I did not answer him, but somewhere on the bench I heard a few disheartened joyless yeses. I looked at L.C. to see if he was one of them, but he was not. He nodded his head like the humble four-year-old that he was while swinging his feet. The kind gentle man then turned to me and asked again, "Would you like to hear it?" I hesitated for a few seconds then reluctantly answered under my breath, "Yes."

"Great!" the man said. "Now, right here in my hand is a camera!" We all turned our heads to look at the camera. We had seen it earlier and had no idea what it was. The man went on.

"What this does is take a picture of you and you," he said randomly pointing at us.

LC and I exchanged a look of uncertainty. We had never had our picture taken nor had we ever seen a camera. Neither of us knew what the soft-spoken man meant, but he kept talking. "The pictures I take of you will be part of the local news," he went on, continuing to share his story and his gaze amongst all of us. He seemed excited about his intentions as he continued on with a joyous and high pitched voice, "Our hope is that once the viewing audience sees your pictures some loving family will want to adopt you!"

That was a grave mistake. The joy he thought he was announcing turned out to be the catalyst to send off a unison of cries. Sobbing sounds filled the air.

"...and take us home with them?" I whined softly.

"Yes," the man replied sorrowfully.

"Not my own family? My mother?"

The man immediately turned his head, putting his attention on me and answered, "No, not your family or your mother."

Just then L.C. burst into tears. I looked around the nice man's thick, brownish-colored hair and saw my little brother crying. I started crying all over again right along with him. The nice gentleman looked down the row of innocent faces, threw back his head, and released a heavy sigh. Mrs. Jo rushed to where we were and kneeled down between us soon after the nice gentleman moved over.

"Look," she says as she scanned the dreary looking faces to her right and then to her left of her. "I thought we already got it straight between all of you that you're here because you are loved. I thought I made that clear."

"Being taken out of our homes and placed among strangers is loved." I thought. Mrs. Jo sounded as if she was just finding a way to get us through this picture taking ordeal, and lying to us was her ticket. It seemed as if she was growing tired of dealing with us, because she ran her hands through her hair and released a heavy sigh just as the photographer had done earlier. What she didn't know was that we were tired of dealing with her as well. We wanted to go home so we could stop traveling from place to place meeting all these strangers.

I thought over the events that led me to this moment, my mother giving us away, my father being killed, and now I'm alone with strange children being put on the auction block. The tears continued to come, and Mrs. Jo was getting sick of them. She glared at my pouting lips, and immediately she addressed me.

"No more tears young man!" she snapped pointing her thin, white finger in my direction. "You either take this picture so that we can run it on tonight's news in hopes of finding you a permanent home, or you will be moving from one adoption agency to another. Do you get it?"

"Yes," I said quietly through the tears and pain

nodding my head at the same time. She waited a few seconds to see if what she had said to me had taken root. I now understood the importance of the picture being taken of me, my brother, and the other children. It was to auction us off on the evening news for all of Mississippi to see. I wanted a permanent place to call home, but the idea of having my picture on television was not something I wanted at all.

"Okay," she said while standing to her feet. She brought our attention to the freshly pressed clothes I had noticed earlier. "Just over there is a table that has pants and shirts for the boys and jumpers and shirts for the girls. These clothes are for you all to wear when taking your pictures. We have done our best to have your correct size. If not, we will adjust the fit long enough for your picture to be taken. Do we understand?"

"Yes," most of us children said.

"Great! It is important that we have your full cooperation so that we can get this done quickly and without much hassle. Mr. Bob can be on his way, and we can get your lovely pictures posted on television tonight. We'll pray some family sees these lovely pictures and want to take you home."

Click! The flash from the camera was bright causing both mine and LC's eyes to shut tight and snatch our heads away from the camera. The photograph was taken, and we moved on for the next orphan.

"I wish we were home," L.C. whined as we climbed down from the chair we had been placed in for our pictures to be taken.

"Stop wishing," I snapped. "Wishing will not get us back home. I've already tried that. Do you know how many times I have wished the same thing? It ain't gonna happen. We don't have a home! So get used to it!" That was the first time I'd been mean to my little brother through this entire horrible ordeal. I was turning into a mean person, and there was nothing anyone could do to stop.

"Would you two like to go outside and play?" Mrs. Jo asked. "The sun is shining and it might dry up some of that blues you're having."

"What does blues mean?" I pondered silently.

"What's blues?" L.C. wanted to know.

We both waited on Mrs. Jo to answer. "It's the sadness that I see in your eyes," she explained as she looked at us intently, scanning me first, then LC, then me again. "I know you are hurting. I can feel your pain. Once those pictures are broadcast this evening on the news, hopefully, someone will fall in love with your handsome faces and invite you both to come live with them." She finished with a big smile and grabbed on to my hand then my brother's. "Let's enjoy this beautiful day. There's only a matter of time, and you will be loved by someone."

Mrs. Jo led my brother and me, as well as the rest of the children through the double doors outside onto the spacious lawn. I remember the sun shining so bright I had to shield my eyes. I heard my brother laugh; removing my hand in disbelief I saw a big smile across his lips. He had already found a simple joy, skipping rocks. He laughed as he watched the pebbles skip across the yard landing not far from where his short arm had thrown them.

I figured if throwing a pebble made him laugh it would do the same for me. After all, we had done a lot of rock throwing when we lived at home in the country. In fact, we threw rocks, not pebbles. At the time we didn't know the difference, they were all rocks to us.

"I bet I can throw farther than you," L.C. said chuckling, his small hand already in throwing form.

I chuckled, too. "I bet you can't," I said to him.

Neither of us had anything to place a bet on so we omitted that part.

"Go ahead. Pick up your rock," he told me going from a chuckle to a laugh.

I was happy to oblige, so I reached down, picked up a rock, and pulled my short arm back ready to let it fly. Just then I heard a male voice shout, "Hey! Cut that out! You might break this glass door!"

He was too late, the rock was in midair. It sought another target, and it wasn't the glass door. It was worse. The girl with the freckled face and red matching hair yelled out. She was the target, and everyone gathered around her as she placed her hand over her right eye holding it tight. Mrs. Jo ran over to see what had happened.

LC quickly dropped the pebble he was about to throw, while I waited for someone to come and yell at me for my unacceptable behavior.

"I knew it!" Mr. Bob, the photographer shouted, coming in our direction. Our eyes flew wide open in fright not knowing what he was about to do to us next. It was obvious he was angry at what I had done.

"Now you have gone and made trouble for yourself," Mr. Bob scolded looking down at me.

From Persecution To Praise

Before long Mrs. Jo walked the victim of my pebble throwing right up to me. She looked down at me shaking her head. I looked up, but was too afraid to look into her eyes so I dropped my stare. "Look at me, Cedric," she said in a stern voice.

Slowly, I looked up still not wanting to meet her eyes. Instead I gazed sorrowfully at the young girl's face. Clearly, the pebble had hit her in the eye. It was already turning blue, red, and green.

"Lucky for both of you …" said Mrs. Jo speaking to LC and me. "…her eye appears to be okay, but it could've been worse. You owe her an apology."

I refused to apologize. So, I said nothing.

"Cedric, do you hear me?" Mrs. Jo said coming closer to me in an intimidating fashion.

Still, I said nothing. I refused to apologize.

"Sorry." LC muddled.

Mrs. Jo turned her attention away from me to LC. "The only role you played in the matter was throwing pebbles, but you did not throw the one that hurt Emily."

"But I'm saying sorry for my brother." He pleaded for me. "He didn't mean to do it …to hurt her."

"I'm going to give you one more chance to tell Emily

that you are sorry for what you did to her. If not you will not like the consequences. I'm going to make you pay."

My tongue was frozen to the roof of my mouth from rage. My only desire was to go home. I stared hard at the little girl whose cry had turned into a whimper. My eyes traveled from Mrs. Jo's waistline up to her chest, her neck, and then her very red lips. I stopped them there as I debated in my mind how I wanted to express this utter contempt. My already corrupt mind dared me to meet her stare with a stare, and I cooperated and did as it requested. Angrily, I met her stare with eyes full of fire.

"I guess you don't mind facing the consequences then, young man."

"I don't!" I snapped.

Out of nowhere Mr. Bob the photographer charged towards me. "That's why nobody wants you!" he barked angrily.

This frightened my little brother, so he came to my defense. "No! Sir! Please don't hurt my brother," he yelled between sobbing and extending his short arms in an attempt to push the man away from me.

"No, one is going to hurt anyone," Mrs. Jo said directing her glare at me. "We just thank God that Emily is okay." She said while turning to look at Emily who had stopped crying and was now sucking her thumb—her way of comforting herself.

LC calmed down and remained silent. I stood there silent and defiant. I had no voice, but I could still make a stand. Suddenly catching me off guard, the photographer snatched me up. He reached down and pushed his thick hand under my elbow while saying, "Come go with me." He lifted me up from the ground as he spoke.

"Just a minute!" Mrs. Jo interjected. "This has nothing to do with you. You're just the photographer."

"Well someone needs to do something about this little out of control brat! He could've put her eye out!"

"But he did not," Mrs. Jo replied respectfully. "Emily is okay, and I will take care of punishing Cedric."

I crossed my hands over my chest, poked my bottom lip out, and looked up at Mrs. Jo defiantly.

"Look at how he is looking at you!" He said even more aggressively. "I ought to…!" he stated reaching out to hit me. I wasn't moved. "Don't you dare touch me!" I scoffed. Mrs. Jo came to my defense. "Look, Mr. Bob please leave the situation alone," She pleaded incessantly.

He began to simmer down, running his thick white

hand across his very bald head. "I just can't stand for kids to act like this. Can't you see this boy is out of control?"

"What I see Mr. Bob is a kid who has lost both his mother and his father and the home he was so comfortable with up until a week or so ago. Can't you see he is hurting? Can't you see that he feels all alone and defenseless against a man…a man your size?"

All of us kids understood. We along with Mrs. Jo stood waiting for the answer Mr. Bob would respond with. No one uttered a word just looked on with eyes longing for compassion. It must have sunk in, because he finally responded with, "Yes. I see."

Something was happening inside of me and no one standing in this large crowd could see it. The spirit of rebellion was after me and it had a strong foothold. Inside I was becoming more and more defiant; more and more intolerant of how people treated me; and more and more stubborn. I was determined, that day, to not be mistreated ever again. I was quickly learning that once the protection of your mother and father is gone you have to protect yourself. That was exactly what I was going to do.

A New Home

I ached as I thought of my mother's face, her patched clothes and her shabby shawl. I wished with all of my heart that I could climb onto her lap, lay my head in her chest, close my eyes, and let the sound of her beating heart lull me to sleep. The thought of being back at home paraded heavily across my mind invading every other thought that wished to come through. Feeling sorry for myself and my brother, tears begin to swell behind my eyes again. I opened and closed them several times in an attempt to fight them from sliding down either of my cheeks. I dared them to spill over. I had started to associate weakness with tears. I would not confess to being weak at all. I was able to gulp back the sob that rose in my throat and went back to sleep.

Morning seemed to come as soon as I had closed my eyes. Still, I was glad to see the sun's rays slipping through the creases in the closed blinds when my eyes finally did come open. The birds were singing as I sat up on my elbows, yawned wide, and looked over at L.C. who appeared to still be sleeping.

I loved the dawning of a new day and hated, absolutely hated, the night. It was during the night that I missed my mother and home more than any other time of the day. It was lonesome without her. It was hurting without her, and it seemed to me that the night hours had that effect on me. The night hours were long, and it seemed I could never sleep through the entire night no matter how I wished to do so. Avoiding waking up during those dark hours was what I wished to do, but it never happened quite like that. I would wake up at 1:00 a.m., then at 3:00 a.m., and then again at 5:00 a.m. Maybe not having enough sleep contributed to my stubbornness as well.

"Rise and shine sleepy heads!" Mrs. Jo sounded off entering the room with just a knocks notice.

"Mrs. Jo!" I said excited to see someone who I thought cared something for me even if it was not much.

"Good news!" she announced smiling big.

From Persecution To Praise

"What?!" I wanted to know.

"The idea to place you and your brother's faces on television the other evening has paid off!"

"You sound excited!" I told her getting more and more excited too. "Tell me what happened, Mrs. Jo!"

"Well, last evening just before Miss. Vicky, my receptionist, left she put a call through to me!"

"Okay," I said anxiously.

"On the phone were Mr. and Mrs. Clemons from Fulton!"

Mrs. Jo was still excited. The tone in her voice spoke volumes.

"And?" I said.

"And they are willing to open the doors of their home to you and L.C.!"

"Did someone call my name?" L.C. asked waking up and rubbing the sleep from his eyes.

"Yes, big boy!" Mrs. Jo announced reaching over and tickling L.C. just under his tiny ribs. He giggled a little. "I called your name!"

"What did you call my name for?" he asked in a whisper.

"... to share with you the good news!" Mrs. Jo told

him.

"What good news?" L.C. pushed gazing directly in Mrs. Jo's direction.

"That you and your brother have a new family and a new home!" Mrs. Jo said making sure she kept the tone in her voice high-pitched and excited.

"Who are they?" L.C. wanted to know. The tone in his voice was low and sad just the opposite of what Mrs. Jo expected.

"What happened to the cheery L.C. that I just tickled?" Mrs. Jo wanted to know hoping to bring him back to the place he was in when she tickled him and he giggled.

For a moment there was silence. Then I murmured, "When do we leave?"

"Today! As soon as you can get up, get breakfast, and get dressed! We will be on our way!"

"And what way is that?" I wanted to know sad but glad at the same time.

"I thought you would be happy about the news!" Mrs. Jo said to me obviously noticing the sadness in my tone and facial expression.

"I am. But I also know that there is no chance of us going back to our own home and mom if we're going some-place else to live with another family."

What I said to Mrs. Jo wiped the broad toothy smile right off of her pale face. The high-pitched voice was reduced to a simple whisper.

"Cedric, I'm doing the very best I can with the hand I've been dealt. I didn't put you in foster care. It was a decision your mother made. I had nothing to do with it. My job, though, as your social worker, is to seek out the best home to place you and your brother in so that you are loved and well taken care of. Then my job is done, and I can move on to the next child, and hopefully do the same for that child as I'm doing for you and your brother."

I could see the seriousness in her eyes, and I could hear the genuineness in the tone of her voice. After all she had shown L.C. and me nothing but love right along with Mr. Loftin. Still, I didn't understand all of the details involved in the system, and because of that, I was suddenly overcome with fear.

"But who are these folks?" I wanted to know feeling apprehensive about going to live with them.

"They are a nice black couple who lives in Fulton and have a big heart for children like you and L.C. They are anxious to see you guys and begin to make friends with you."

"I don't want to be their friend," L.C. said pouting.

"Okay, you two," Mrs. Jo begin sounding a lot more serious. "Would you rather continue to travel from place to place, from one agency to another, meeting more strangers or would you rather be placed in a home that has a mother and a father and lots of love, and who wants you so much to be a part of their family? The choice is yours."

Again a silence fell over the room while Mrs. Jo waited for an answer. L.C. and I mulled over what the answer would be.

"Okay, Mrs. Jo," I finally said submitting to whatever family she had chosen for us.

"Okay, what?" she asked looking directly into my eyes.

"Okay. We want to go live with Mr. and Mrs. Clemons in…" I couldn't remember the town she had earlier mentioned they lived. She repeated it.

"In Fulton." She paused for a minute then released a heavy sigh before going on. "Okay, let's get up and get on the road. We have a family that's waiting to see you two."

Mr. Loftin brought the sedan that they were riding in to a complete stop just in front of a large red-bricked home with black, weathered shutters. The Clemons must have either known the exact time we were arriving at their home, or they had great intuition because they were waiting on the large porch their arms stretched out to embrace the both of us.

"Mr. and Mrs. Clemons this is Cedric!" Mrs. Jo announced excitedly.

"Aaww, looky here, looky here!" the short, caramel-colored woman said with a wide smile. She pulled me tight into her thick left side. I buried my face there.

"And this is his little brother, L.C.!" Mrs. Jo continued with the same excitement.

Mrs. Clemons repeated the same words, "Aaww, looky here, looky here!" she said pulling L.C. into a tight hug as well, burying his face into her thick right side.

"Ain't they handsome, honey?!" Mrs. Clemons said to Mr. Clemons who stood there with a big smile. He embraced the both of us shortly after we disengaged our faces from his wife's thick side.

Mr. Clemons towered over us. He was about six feet tall or more. His skin was walnut-colored and his black hair grayed at either of his temples. His moustache was gray as well.

I threw my eyes first at Mrs. Clemons, then at Mr.

Clemons their smiles seemed convincing, but I looked at the both of them through the lenses of distrust. We did not know them from any of the many other strangers we had met along the way. No one at the moment was able to stop that tape of insecurity from playing over and over and over in my mind.

Suddenly an overwhelming feeling of dependency washed all over me from my head to my toe. I knew there was no one left to depend on but the Clemons. Mrs. Jo was on her way to somewhere else leaving both me and L.C. with the Clemons.

Before she left however, she turned to me and spoke through ruby red colored lips. "These two people here, Mr. and Mrs. Clemons, are two of the finest people you guys ever wanted to meet. You can trust them to love you and take care of you as if you were their own. You won't ever be alone again. Isn't that right?" Mrs. Jo finished her thought then turned first to Mr. Clemons then to Mrs. Clemons and waited for them to confirm what she had just announced to the boys.

"Absolutely!" Mr. Clemons said out loud while his wife nodded in agreement, a broad smile on her face.

Both L.C. and I looked at the couple as we were being

From Persecution To Praise

reassured by their agreements. Mrs. Jo went on.

"Now here take this," she said.

I looked down at what she was handing to me. It was a small white envelope in her hands. Slowly, I reached out and took the envelope into my small hands and proceeded to open it. I pulled out of the envelope a slip of folded paper. As I unfolded it, L.C. came and stood beside me peering over my left shoulder. It was obvious that Mrs. Jo knew I could hardly read and that L.C. could not read at all. So, once again she opened her ruby-red lips and said, "That's my number both at my home and at the office. If either of you need anything, anything at all, please don't hesitate to call me."

Both L.C. and I looked up at Mrs. Jo. We could see seriousness in the eyes that stared back at us. We believed her and took her word for it. She then turned her attention away from us and put it back on Mr. and Mrs. Clemons who were standing by observing. She pushed her hand first in the direction of the wife and then in the direction of the husband. "That goes for the both of you as well," she told us them.

"So long," she said to us all before pivoting on the high heels of her black shiny pumps and heading for the car where Mr. Loftin sat talking on the phone waiting for her.

The Clemons, L.C., and I stood on the porch of the large red-bricked home watching Mrs. Jo's back as she swung her hips while she walked. Inside of the car, while buckling up, she peered through the window and with a big smile on her face waved good-bye along with Mr. Loftin who had remained in the car completing the paper work for the Department of Human Services.

"Well boys it's time to see your room!" Mrs. Clemons exclaimed. She turned to enter the opened door held by Mr. Clemons. He waited while Mrs. Clemons went through the door. I followed closely on her heels, while L.C. followed closely on mine. Mr. Clemons followed behind us all closing the door.

Hearing the door close behind me sent me into some sort of tantrum. Out of nowhere panic filled my heart.

"Noooooo!" I yelled falling to the floor. Large hot tears streamed quickly down my face. These emotions had been brewing inside of me since leaving Jackson, but I had tried, as usual, to keep it all together. Whatever the it was.

Immediately, Mr. Clemons went to where I had fallen and stood over me with a seriously concerned look on his aging face.

From Persecution To Praise

"What's the matter, boy?!" he wanted to know. His black-with-gray, thick eyebrows came together as he bent his back in the direction of me. I either did not hear what he said or had chosen to ignore him. I don't remember.

"What's the matter, boy?!" he asked, yet again, staring down at me, his wrinkled hands now resting on his weak knees.

"Wait a minute, honey," Mrs. Clemons softly said stepping around her husband.

"Okay," Mr. Clemons replied straightening his back, but keeping his stare on me lying on the floor having a fit.

"I know how much you are hurting, baby," Mrs. Clemons said continuing in the same soft tone with a slight bend to her aging back.

My body shook in a deep, long shudder. Mrs. Clemons could tell the tone she intentionally put in her voice was having a major impact on me because I was now fighting back the tears.

L.C., in one swift move, came from behind Mr. Clemons, pushing by Mrs. Clemons, fell next to me.

"It's okay, brother," he said his tiny voice cracking. "Everything gone be alright. Okay? Okay, brother?"

All three of them patiently waited to see how I was

going to respond to Mrs. Clemons' and L.C.'s pleas. It took a few minutes, however, the wait was worth it because the tears stopped flowing, and I sat up. A final sigh, laced with one more disappointment, came up my throat.

"Come on baby. Let me show you your room," Mrs. Clemons said breaking the silence that had suddenly surrounded us. She straightened her back and stepped aside.

Mr. Clemons brushed softly past her and gently reached out aging hand and waited for me to extend mine. He was the head of that household and Mrs. Clemons knew and respected it. Mr. Clemons noticed my eyes falling on his outstretched hand. At first I did not take it. I was still wrestling with trusting him and his wife. Finally, I slowly brought my hand up from resting beside me and gently placed it inside of his.

Firmly, but not intimidatingly, Mr. Clemons closed his hand around my hand. It was a sign he had me, and I could trust both him and his wife to be there for L.C. and me.

"So, are you boys ready for the time of your lives?!" Mr. Clemons wanted to know putting excitement in his voice.

"I'm read…read…ready," I stuttered trying to believe

what he was saying, but I didn't.

My Visitation From Daddy

"Cedric! Cedric! Wake up! You're dreaming!"

I struggled to a sitting position as L.C.'s childish voice not only penetrated the dark-covered room, but also my dream. I brought my curled fists to my closed eyes and rubbed the sleep out of them. L.C. laughed a little.

"What's funny?!" I asked sternly, slightly pushing L.C. away from me.

"You, you up here making all types of crazy sounds!"

We slept on bunk beds purchased especially for us. Mr. and Mrs. Clemons had made the purchase the minute they found out that L.C. and I were coming to stay. I was awarded my wish to have the top bunk, because I was the oldest and it was my request. L.C. wanted it, too. The Clemons decided to toss a coin to make the decision fair. I called tails and L.C. called heads. Tails had won, and I was happy about it. However, I was not so happy about being awaken from my dream by LC.

"You messed up my dream!" I said to L.C. dissatisfied with his uninvited interruption. He had shaken me out of my sleep and away from my dream.

"I'm sorry," L.C. told me bringing his hint of laughter to an end after noticing my annoyance with him.

"Come on. Sit right here," I told my brother smoothing out a spot on the blanket for him to sit.

"Why? What for?" L.C. wanted to know.

"I want to tell you about something that happened when we lived with Auntie before going to Jackson."

"What?" L.C. asked sitting in the spot on the blanket that I had smoothed for him to sit, his thin eyebrows coming together in an inquisitive fashion.

"Okay," I told him lowering my voice to a whisper. I could barely see my brother's face in the dark room. He knew I was there, though.

"Now, tell me what happened before we left Auntie's house?" L.C. said, revisiting the subject of conversation.

"Well, one night after everyone had gone to sleep, I was laying on my bed in the dark."

"Okay," L.C. said.

"I was crying. I had been locked away in the room all day, and I didn't want to come out."

"I remember that, Cedric."

"The room was completely dark. I will never forget. I felt someone touch my feet."

"What?!" L.C. said his voice raising.

"Shhh!" I said reaching my hand out in the dark to touch his mouth."

"Sorry, brother. You know I got a big mouth," L.C. confessed.

"I know that you do too," I whispered. "But we don't want to wake up the whole house."

"I know. I know. Go on with your story."

L.C. shifted on the blanket until he was comfortable. I decided to wait until he had stopped moving before continuing with the story about the dream.

"Well about the same time someone touched my feet I heard a voice."

"What did the voice say?" L.C. pushed.

"It said, 'son it's going to be okay. I am with you.'"

"You think it was daddy?!" L.C. said his tone filled with excitement.

"Yes," I answered before going on. "The voice

belonged to our daddy."

"Wow!" L.C. responded. "Tell me more. Please!"

"Yes, there was a sudden feeling of peace that I felt."

"But Cedric, weren't you scared?" L.C. wanted to know.

"A little bit. But I felt more peace than I did fear. It was like daddy was speaking directly to me."

"Where was I at when this happened?"

"L.C. I think you were in the next room sleeping," I told my little brother growing annoyed at his interruptions.

"Tell me more, Cedric."

"I will," I snapped my tone going up an octave. "If you will stop interrupting!"

"Shhh!" L.C. said reaching his hand out to cover my mouth just as I had done to him earlier in the conversation.

I drew in a deep breath laced with impatience and went on.

"After that I slowly climbed off the bed and went to the door. I opened it carefully and peeped out to be sure no one else was up but me."

"Was Auntie up?" L.C. asked.

"No, Auntie was not up. So I walked into the living room and it was then that I noticed a glow coming from a certain spot on the couch."

"Oh, my goodness, Cedric. You're scaring me."

"Don't be scared. No one is going to hurt you."

"Promise?!" L.C. asked.

"Promise," I reassured him.

"Where was the glow coming from?"

"At first I thought it was coming from the lamp on the table next to the couch, but that light was not on."

"And?"

"Then I thought the glow might have come from outside from the moon."

"It didn't?"

"No, L.C. it didn't."

"Then where do you think it came from?"

"I think it was a glow from our daddy. I think the glow was our daddy."

"Really?"

"Yes, L.C. really."

"What did you do then?" L.C. pushed.

"I walked across the floor, got up on the couch and lay in the glow."

"You did what?!"

"Yes, L.C. I walked across the floor, got up on the

couch and lay in the glow."

I noticed L.C. move closer toward me. He got so close I could feel his breath on my face.

"Don't be scared little brother. Daddy wouldn't hurt us."

"I know. But I'm still scared."

"Well, I guess he wouldn't because I believe that was him glowing in the dark and I just lay in the spot and went to sleep."

"Brother you are so brave."

"No, I'm not so brave. I just know that daddy was letting me know that no matter where you and I went he would be with us."

A hush filled the dark room. I was trying to remember all of the details of the dream. It had been so real to me, and I didn't want to leave the tiniest moment out. It was my reassurance that no matter what I would face, my daddy would be there with me if in spirit only.

"Cedric," L. C. started.

"Yes."

"Why does no one want us?"

The hurt and pain I thought I had suppressed suddenly come flooding back into my emotions like a tidal wave knocking me off of my peacefulness.

I swallowed hard, opening and closing my eyes, trying to keep the lump that was now lodged in my throat and the tears that were threating to come at bay. I wanted and needed to be strong for my brother. After a few minutes, I told him.

"The Clemons want us."

With that said, L.C. crawled into my lap, laid his head on my shoulder and fell fast asleep. I wrapped my short arms as far around him as they would go hoping to calm any of his fears and trim any amount of his insecurities. Soon, after staring into the dark room at nothing in particular, left completely and totally with my thoughts, I fell asleep as well..

Gaining a Family

L.C.'s screaming jolted me right out of my slumber. Quickly, I jerked my head in his direction.

"Look!" he said panting as if he had ran a marathon.

Even though it was now morning and the sun's rays broke through the opening in the curtain I struggled to gain complete control of my sight.

"What is it?!" I asked, my eyes widening in horror while following the direction of his pointed finger. We clung tightly to each other trembling just a bit. Our eyes stayed on the two unexpected guests that were standing on the floor below the top bunk where we were sleeping.

Just then Mrs. Clemons came rushing into the room.

"I thought I told you two to go to the breakfast table!" she said her voice pitched high as she stared down at the two young girls about the same age as me.

Both L.C. and I looked over at Mrs. Clemons with a confused but relieved look. It was apparent to us that at least she knew who they were.

In the light, thrown off by the sun's rays, I noticed one girl was taller than the other. But both were the color of Mrs. Clemons—a smooth caramel brown. They both also had two long pigtails hanging on either side of their thin faces.

Once we realized they were not ghosts, but actual living and breathing human beings, L.C. and I slowly relaxed our tight hug.

"Good morning, boys," Mrs. Clemons said lowering her voice and putting a smile on her face at the same time.

My stare met hers as I received her morning salutation and I said back to her, "Good morning, Mrs. Clemons."

Both girls simultaneously brought their tiny hands to cover their mouths and let out giggles. Immediately, my attention, followed by L.C.'s went from Mrs. Clemons back to the two unknown girls.

Mrs. Clemons put her attention on the two girls as well and smiled a hint of a smile.

"What's so funny?" L.C. wanted to know asking me rather than them.

"You called her 'Mrs. Clemons!'" the taller girl said bringing her giggle to an end and pointing at the lady in the red, blue and green floral duster.

L.C. and I exchanged a confused look.

"What are we supposed to call her then?" I wanted to know.

"Yeah, she's Mrs. Clemons to us. That's what Mrs. Jo, our social worker, told us to call her," L.C. chided in.

The shorter of the two girls laughed out loud bending at the waist as she did it. The taller of the two girls looked at the shorter of the two girls and started to laugh out loud right along with her. Within seconds, Mrs. Clemons started laughing. The laughing grew louder and louder between the trio.

I brought my shoulders up then down when I noticed L.C. looking at me with the same confused look he had moments ago. "I don't know why they are laughing. So don't ask me again."

The laughing went on for several seconds before Mrs. Clemons reached out and gently touched them both on their small shoulders. Then Mrs. Clemons looked up at the two of us and gave us a long, silent look before speaking with a loving softness. "I guess they thought calling me

'Mrs. Clemons' was too formal."

"Do you all know something that we don't?" I asked looking at the taller girl first and then to the shorter girl next.

"She's our Bigmama!" the shorter girl said pointing at the older woman in the room.

I looked at L.C. and L.C. looked at me. We both mouthed the word Bigmama at the same time. Suddenly, L.C. burst into laughter at the word. "Bigmama?! What's a Bigmama?!" he asked looking at me yet again to answer a question I had no answer for.

Within just a few seconds, due to L.C.'s crazy-sounding laughter, I started to laugh as well. "I don't know what a Bigmama is!"

Down on the floor the taller girl and the shorter girl stood staring up at us with their arms folded across their chests and Mrs. Clemons stood beside them staring up at us with either of her hands resting on her large hips. All three were stoned-faced watching us laugh out loud. Mrs. Clemons allowed us to laugh as loud and as much as we wanted to. I figured she believed we had not had a good laugh since we were born and boy was she right—we had not. Still, the taller girl thought we had overdone it and called us out on it.

"Okay, you two. Nothing's funny about calling my grandmother, Bigmama."

"Bigmama!" L.C. sounded out and continued to laugh hard.

"Stop it!" I said correcting his behavior after noticing the seriousness on the taller girl's face.

Finally, he brought his laughter to an end just as I had. After a brief moment of silence, Mrs. Clemons spoke up. "Boys, yes, these are my granddaughters and they do call me Bigmama!"

L.C. turned his head in my direction to see if he had my permission to laugh again. I elbowed him in his side and shook my head no.

"This is Jennetta who is the same age as you, Cedric. Eight. And this is Jas who is five."

"Hi!" Jas said with a smile, waving her hand. Jennetta said nothing. She waved her hand, though.

L.C. looked at me as if he needed permission to speak back. "Go ahead," I told him. "Speak."

"Hi," he said. His tone lacked excitement.

"Nice to meet you!" I responded making sure I put enough excitement in my tone for myself and to make up for L.C.'s lack of. My hope was that if we were nice enough and behaved in a friendly manner maybe we would be acceptable and stay in this home forever.

"Great!" Mrs. Clemons started looking up at L.C. and me. "Now that we have formally introduced ourselves let's get one thing straight right now before God and everybody."

"Who's God?" L.C. wanted to know.

Hurriedly, Mrs. Clemons answered his question. "Glad you asked. We have a Bible lesson every Thursday evening rights here in this here house of mine, and you're in luck to find out who God is because this evening is the Thursday evening."

"You mean to tell me you guys have never heard of God?!" Jennetta wanted to know, her eyebrows rose to them.

I opened my mouth to answer her question, but Mrs. Clemons stepped in. Tiny lines of frustration creased her forehead. "Stop it, Jennetta. That's not right, and you know it."

"Well, I was just asking a question," the young girl added crossing and reclosing her arms.

"And don't give me no attitude young lady," Mrs.

Clemons snapped.

"I'm not Bigmama. It's just…"

"It's just nothing. Now get in the kitchen and help your grandfather with breakfast."

Mrs. Clemons finished with her statement and cut her eyes first at Jennetta then at Jas before replying emphatically, "You, too, Jas!" The girls knew their Bigmama meant business. They did not tarry another moment, but backed out of the conversation and the room all at the same time.

L.C. chuckled behind the girl's backs as they hurriedly exited the room. Again, I elbowed L.C. in his side. I did not want anything to go wrong and ruin the chance of being told we had to leave from yet another home.

"Okay. Okay," L.C. whispered.

"Lord, you children are something else," Mrs. Clemons said as she laughed a little. She stopped her small laughter just as quick as she had started it and looked up seriously and genuinely at L.C. and me. She went on. "You two don't know how happy my husband and I are to have you join our family. When I saw your little faces on the television I knew that I was supposed to call the number they gave." Mrs. Clemons inhaled and exhaled and continued to speak to us. "I know what it's like to have no mother and father. I was right where y'all are, no one to love me but God. God stepped right in on time and a wonderful, loving family took me in and raised me as their own. Never will I forget that. I told the Lord that one day, if he gave me the strength, I would do the same thing for other children. Look at what God did. He brought you to me, and I'm so thankful that he gave me enough house and enough love for the both of you and my grands! What a mighty good God we serve! I'm going to tell you all about Him. Okay?"

"Yes, ma'am," I answered. L.C. said nothing. Mrs. Clemons finished up her thought by saying. "You boys are at home. Whatever me and my husband got here ain't none of it too good for you. You're welcome to it. All I ask is that you be obedient and do as me and your Bigdaddy say. That ain't too much to ask for. Those are just expectations. By the way, from this moment forward, I'm no longer Mrs. Clemons to you. I'm Bigmama. That man there in that kitchen cooking our breakfast is no longer Mr. Clemons to you. He's your Bigdaddy. We expect to be called that. This makes us family. Alright?"

As the conversation ended so did much of the fear and

apprehension that was in the pit of my stomach. Her kind words and the tone in which she spoke them put me at complete ease.

"Now get down off that bed and wash your face and brush your teeth and meet your family in about five minutes!"

A House Of Prayer

L.C. and I entered the bathroom just doors down from where we had slept and washed up. Bigmama had given L.C. a navy blue toothbrush and to me a dark green toothbrush the night before.

"Brush them teeth good," she had reminded us while handing each of us a very white wash cloth. "Teeth got to last you a long time."

I watched as L.C. brought his toothbrush back and forth—back and forth—across his short upper teeth then his short lower teeth. It appeared to me that he was doing a pretty good job getting them cleaned.

"Now spit that out of your mouth!" I told him as the white toothpaste foamed around his tiny mouth and began to slip out of either corner.

He did just as I had requested. He spit. However, the toothpaste from his mouth landed all over the sink.

"Clean it up!" I demanded. "Right now!" I wanted to make sure we did everything right. I wanted no reason found to throw us out or take us back to the adoption agency.

Quickly, L.C. took his very white wash cloth, held it under the running cold water before squeezing as much of the water out of it that his strength would allow him to.

"Now go on. Wipe that off the sink."

L.C. did.

"Now wash your face," I went on. Of course as I was directing him to brush his teeth and wash his face, I was doing the exact same thing. Looking around, I noticed through the mirror on the door, the reflection of some boys clothing lying across the bed. There was underwear, pants, shirt, and socks lying across L.C.'s bed and the same was lying across my bed. We both rushed out of the bathroom and right up to either of our beds and snatched the clothes.

"Wow, new clothes!" I exclaimed with excitement and wide eyes. I held the dark-colored pants up to me.

"Look at my shirt!" L.C. exclaimed with the same

excitement and wide eyes holding his shirt up to his body as well.

"So, I see you like your new clothes," a female voice said. Since the voice was unfamiliar and startled us, so we jerked our heads in that direction.

"Hi, my name is Barbara. I'm Mr. and Mrs. Clemons' daughter. I could hardly wait to meet the two of you," the woman said with a big smile.

L.C. and I exchanged a look laced with confusion and fear.

"You don't have to be afraid of me. I'm only here to help you two boys get adjusted and help my parents give you the best home that they possibly can."

L.C. and I exchanged yet another look. This time it was laced with joy. We both then put our stares on her along with a smile.

"Great! It's so good to see you two smile! I think you might have met my little girl already!"

I brought my shoulders up then down—uncertain.

"She was in your room earlier. My mother told me she and her first cousin, Jas, scared you guys!" Barbara finished her thought and then chuckled.

"Yes!" L.C. said putting enthusiasm in his voice. "She

was the tall one!"

Barbara continued to chuckle. "Yes, she is tall for an eight-year-old. She gets that from her father."

"So, the girl's name is Jen..Jen..," I stumbled trying to remember and pronounce her name simultaneously.

"Jennetta! Her name is Jennetta. And yes that is my baby girl." Barbara replied.

"You just have one child?" I pushed.

"Yes. One is enough. I help out with Jas who is my sister's daughter," the lady went on, bringing her chuckle to an end.

"Where does she live?" L.C. asked.

"Here. Right here with our parents."

"Where is she right now?" L.C. continued.

"Stop asking all of them questions," I insisted elbowing him in his side.

"No," Barbara said chuckling yet again. "It's no problem. I will be happy to introduce you to her. Come on."

L.C. followed Barbara out of the room, and I followed him. The smell of frying bacon filled the hallway as we made our way toward the front of the large house. Just inside of the living room I noticed a bed with a woman lying in it. I stopped immediately in my tracks—suddenly feeling nervous about meeting this woman and I did not know why.

"What's wrong?" Barbara asked me.

I dropped my head and looked down at the floor.

"Cedric," L.C. started up bending at the waist to look up into my face. "What's wrong?"

"I don't know. I just don't want to meet her."

Just then a weird sound came out of the woman's throat and filled the room. She thrashed about in her bed before rolling over on her side and coming face-to-face with us.

L.C. stopped moving forward at that moment as well while Barbara proceeded forward. At the side of the bed, she stopped, took the woman's hand and said. "Good morning, Joyce!"

Joyce brought her eyes away from L.C. or me and put them directly on her sister's face. She seemed to be excited with wide eyes and an opened mouth to match.

"If you're wondering whether or not she can talk the answer is 'no' she can't," Barbara turned around to tell us.

Neither L.C. nor I went any closer. Just then Bigmama entered the room wiping her hands on the front of her apron. She nudged both L.C. and me forward.

"Come on. I see that you have met your big sister, Barbara. Now it's time you meet your big sister, Joyce."

L.C. looked at me. I looked at L.C. It seemed as if both of our short feet were nailed to the carpeted floor.

"Come on. She won't bite. Will you my baby?!" Bigmama said through a big smile reassuring the pair.

Joyce smiled a big gummy smile at the two boys as their short feet finally moved them forward in her direction. She made a deep-throated moan as they came closer. Her excitement to meet them led her to reach out her hand to them once Barbara let go of it.

"Go on!" Barbara encouraged. "Take her hand Cedric! She is harmless."

Slowly, I reached my hand toward hers until they finally met. She squeezed my little hand, but not hard though and moaned something that I did not understand.

"Joyce," Barbara started. "This is our new little brother, Cedric! Say 'hello' to Cedric!"

Barbara might have been excited but I was not. I was scared of Joyce, even though her gentle handshake spoke volumes—kind, kind, kind. She moved her thick lips that were now coated with saliva as I stood as still as I could and watched her every move ready to run at the drop of a hat.

"See, she won't hurt you! Will you baby?!" Bigmama asked looking lovingly at her daughter.

"Uhh! Uhh!" was the only noise that resembled a word I heard her say.

"L.C.! Come on and meet your big sister!" Bigmama said putting a hint of insistency in her voice this time.

I turned and looked L.C. directly in his eyes. They seemed to beg for my reassurance and immediately after I nodded, he slowly came in the direction of the bed holding Joyce.

"Joyce, meet your little brother, L.C." Barbara said in her introduction.

L.C. brought his tiny hands together in a clasped position after Joyce dropped my hand and reached for his. He held them tightly together, stopped immediately in his tracks and began backing away at the same time.

"Nooo!" he demanded crying out. "I'm scared of her!"

Joyce brought her thick eyebrows together in confusion.

"She doesn't understand why you are afraid of her?" Bigmama said to L.C. "She won't hurt you. Go on. Give her your hand." Bigmama reached down and tried to bring his tightly clutched hands apart. The harder she tried; the harder he fought against it.

"Nooo!"

"Breakfast is ready!" Bigdaddy said loud enough to break the gathering around Joyce's bed. He had entered the room unnoticed.

Immediately, I went to my brother and brought him into a tight, comforting hug. "It's alright little brother," I told him. "It's alright."

"Yes, it's all right, L.C." Barbara said in a comforting tone that resembled mine. She patted L.C. on his back while she led us to the kitchen. Bigmama was right behind us wearing one of her signature dusters.

Just inside of the kitchen L.C. looked over his left shoulder to be sure Joyce had not followed them.

"Don't worry, my son," Bigmama said. "My baby, Joyce, can't walk. She can't use her legs like we can."

"She has M.S.!" Jennetta yelled out. She and Jas were sitting at the kitchen table waiting for breakfast and coloring a picture of something I did not recognize.

"Yes, my mother has not walked in a few years," Jas said sadly looking up from coloring. "She never plays with me. I miss that."

Her sadness moved something inside of me. Remembering the absence of my own mother, and how it made me feel led me to go to her and wrap my short arms around her in an attempt to comfort. And if that did not work, I spoke to her. "It's okay, Jas. I know what it feels like to have a mother that can't play with you. At least you are with your mother in the same house. I have no mother."

"Pancakes are served!" Bigdaddy loudly announced once again breaking up the pity party. It was like he was having none of that.

"Pancakes!" Jennetta said out loud picking up her fork waiting for Bigdaddy to come around to her with the platter of nicely browned flat bread.

Neither L.C. nor I could remember the last time we had eaten pancakes, so we were just as excited about laying our wide eyes on the platter loaded with pancakes as Jennetta.

I glanced around the kitchen. It was so different from the one I remembered back at home. For only an instant I yearned with all of my heart for my own kitchen—my own home—with my brothers, sisters and mother. Then sharply I reminded myself that this place was my home now, and I would do my very best to accept the fact that turning back was not an option for me.

"Here, L.C. take this chair," Bigmama said to my brother putting her hand on the chair she was speaking about. She then turned to me and said. "Cedric this is your chair." The look on her face told me that she was as happy to have us sitting at her table as we were happy to have been offered a seat.

Bigmama sat at one end of the long table while Bigdaddy sat at the other. Barbara sat next to her daughter Jennetta while L.C. and I sat on either side of Jas.

"Let's bow for grace," Bigdaddy said looking down one side of the long table and back up the other side.

Immediately, everyone sitting at the table other than L.C. and me put a bend in their necks, dropped their heads, closed their eyes, and brought their hands together.

"Father God," Bigdaddy started. "Thank you for this beautiful day that you have given us. We thank you for allowing us to see it. We thank you for our new blessings, little Cedric and little L.C. We pray, Father God, that they will find love and comfort in this home. Thank you for everyone seated at this table and bless this food that we are about to receive for the nourishment of our bodies. Once we have eaten and gained the nutrition from it we will use the energy to be a blessing to someone else. In the name of Jesus I do pray. Amen."

"Amen," Bigmama, Bigdaddy, Barbara, Jennetta and Jas said.

Everybody dug into their food once the pancakes had syrup poured on them and the bacon and scrambled eggs were added to their plates.

"Wait just a minute," Bigmama said, interrupting the fellowship intentionally.

All eyes shifted down the table and were put on Bigmama confused by the move she had just made. She put her fork down and opened her mouth to speak. "L.C. and Cedric," she started. "I noticed that while we prayed you two did not. Now in this house we serve the Lord. In this house we pray. In this house we say grace every time we eat."

Both L.C. and I could hear the seriousness about this subject in Bigmama's tone that clearly matched the look on Bigmama's face.

"Do we understand, young men?" Bigmama asked waiting for an answer.

Cedric Doss

"Yes, ma'am," we both answered.

BOYS AND GIRLS

"Fishing?" I asked.

"Yes, fishing!" Bigmama said with excitement. "I love me some fishing! Now, put on these old clothes and meet me and your Bigdaddy at the truck in about ten minutes. Okay?"

"Yes, ma'am."

Bigmama left the room leaving me and L.C. to think about what she had just said.

"Do you like fishing?" L.C. asked me wrinkling his nose.

I brought my shoulders up then down. "I don't know. I've never been fishing before."

"I don't think I'm going to like it. Don't you have to put bugs on the stick?" L.C. continued.

"No, stupid. You have a fishing pole and you put worms on it. You throw it in the water, and wait for a fish to bite it. When it does, pull the fish up on the bank. Put it in the bucket to keep."

L.C. looked puzzled before saying, "I thought you never been fishing before"

"I haven't," I told him.

"Then how do you know so much about it?"

"I heard our daddy talk about it one time."

L.C. watched every word that fell from my lips before saying, "Oh, okay."

L.C. and I dressed in the old clothes Bigmama had left for us. Both shirts were faded red and blue plaid with a tear on the elbows. The old jeans were a faded blue with white patches on either of the knees. The sneakers were obviously old and worn, but the entire outfit was fit only for fishing. All of our other clothes were too nice for that sport.

"You ready?" I asked L.C. as he buttoned the last button on his faded red and blue plaid shirt.

"Yes, I guess."

"Then let's get out of here so that we don't disappoint Bigmama and Bigdaddy."

Out of our room and into the hall L.C. and I went.

"Do you have to use the bathroom before we go?" I asked my little brother.

He stood in the middle of the hall thinking over what I had just asked him.

"Do you?!" I pushed.

"You don't have to raise your voice at me!" L.C. said his tone a hint higher.

"I'm not. Just use the bathroom if you need to."

Without answering me, L.C. darted into the hall bathroom.

"See you at the truck," I called after him.

As I rounded the corner of the house I discovered I was alone. Enjoying the silence, I gladly leaned against a nearby silver leaf tree. The Clemons' land was beautiful. The house overlooked a large meadow dotted with pine trees, a few of them still small; many tall and blowing in the wind. To one side of the meadow lay a field of black soil rising in rows of low mounds. Next to the back of the house was a garden, and I could recognize collard greens and okra growing alongside the other. If only I could show this to my mother and the rest of my family. They would love to know that L.C. and I were now in a home that truly wanted and loved us.

I still missed home, though. The thought of my mother's face paraded across my mind along with the thought of my brother's and sister's faces, too. Vividly, I remembered them all. None of my memory had faded when it came to remembering them. It never would. No matter how loving and accepting Bigmama and Bigdaddy were of L.C. and me, I loved and missed my family. There was no way I could just forget that part of me. It was too important. Those people that I had waved good-bye to a while ago were blood—blood relatives. Suddenly, my vision was blurred. It was because the tears threatened to come. I rushed to put out of my mind the thoughts that I knew would lead to those tears spilling over the rim of my eyes and down either side of my face.

A bright spot of color lying on a patch of grass right near my feet suddenly caught my attention. I bent to pick it up. It was a doll made of an all bright yellow cloth, black hair made of tangled black yarn, and a brown face with big black eyes. I had never seen a doll that looked like that before. The dolls my sisters played with were made of a hard plastic and they all had white-colored faces and very blue eyes. For just a moment I held the doll close.

"What you doing with my doll?!" The mocking voice came from somewhere just behind me.

I whirled to face Jennetta. "Never saw a doll that looked like this before that's all," I mumbled then dropped the doll to the ground.

Jennetta grinned menacingly. "You dropped your dolly, little girl.

"I'm not a little girl!" I said angrily. "I'm not a girl at all for your information!"

I reached up and grabbed Jennetta by the shoulder and pushed her hard backwards. Jennetta was no stranger to fighting. Having learned well from her best friend Mike, how to protect herself, she reacted instinctively. Rushing into me, she butted me in the stomach with her head. She was able to hook her left foot behind mine and with a jerk pulled me down. I landed hard on my back in the dirt.

"What's going on?" L.C. asked coming from around the corner of the house staring at us suspiciously. "Are y'all fighting?"

"No," I answered quickly. "Just having fun."

L.C. looked a little dubious but said, "Bigmama and Bigdaddy ready to go fishing. They're waiting on you at the truck."

As L.C. walked away, Jennetta reached down, grabbed me by the elbow, and pulled me to my feet. Dusting me off much harder than necessary, she chuckled, "Want to talk about dolls again? Or do you have enough sense to talk about something different?"

"But what you get so mad at me about?" I wanted to know desperately. "I was only having a little fun with you. That's all and before I knew it I was on the ground."

Jennetta folder her arms across her chest and looked at me with a look of accomplishment written all over her face.

"I'm not mad at you. I just wanted to see if I could beat you up. You are eight and I am eight. I am a girl and you are a boy. And yes, I can beat you up. This is my Bigmama and Bigdaddy's house. And if you ever think about disrespecting either of them I will bring you right back to this place and kick your butt again. You got that?!"

I did not know whether to speak to the finger she had pointed inches from the tip of my nose or to the angry face she made while speaking, but I did answer her, feeling defeated, "Yes, I got it."

"Cedric! Jennetta! Come on here. The fish are waiting for me!"

It was Bigmama. I inhaled a deep breath and released

it. I felt a sense of comfort seeing her. What Jennetta had done to me was humiliating. I was a boy and she was a girl. A girl was never supposed to beat up a boy. I wanted to cry so bad. On the way to the truck those hot tears that I was so used to crying rushed to the surface of my eyes. Again, I blinked several times as a way to fight them from spilling over. No way would I allow Jennetta see me cry, or allow her to defeat me and reduce me to tears.

THE FEAST OF ALL FEAST

"Help yourself, boys!" Bigmama said with a big grin pushing a paper plate at me and one at L.C. "Children! Everyone come eat!" she shouted to the rest of the crowd of hungry people.

What a feast! At first all I could do was stare at the tables and tables of food. Never in my short life had I ever seen so much food at one time in one place. On one table was all types of meats—ribs, pork chops, roasts, fried chicken, steaks, pig feet and chitterlings. On another table was assorted side dishes—spaghetti, potato salad, fried corn, collard and mustard greens, green beans with ham hocks, sweet potato casserole, chicken spaghetti, and fried okra. On another table was an array of desserts—sweet potato pies, caramel cakes, strawberry short cake topped with whipped cream, chocolate cakes, pecan pies and homemade vanilla ice cream. I closed my eyes and breathed in the wonderful smell of the food. My nostrils stretched as wide as they could while my stomach begged to taste some of it, if not all of it. When I opened my eyes, Jennetta was standing right next to me.

"What do you want?!" I asked with a mix of fear and uncertainty.

"Nothing," she answered matter-of-factly.

"Oh, okay," I replied releasing the sudden onset of tension.

"Bet you never seen this much food before in your whole eight years of living. Have you?!" she asked nudging me to move along.

"Uh, no..no," I stammered.

"You need a few good meals to build those little puny arms."

I remembered what she had done to me some months ago just before going fishing with Bigmama and Bigdaddy. Not only had she whipped me fighting, but she had also whipped me at fishing later the same day. She had caught ten fish to my measly two. She had never let me forget how much better she was at everything than me. I was okay with it. What she did not know was I was never in competition with her. She was a girl. I was a boy.

The rest of the children had carried their plates loaded with all types of food to the carport that had been designated just for us. The men took their plates to the inside of the house. From where I sat in the carport I could hear the low, rumble of their conversations with an occasional outburst of laughter. The women did not sit anywhere particular, especially Bigmama. She bustled back and forth between the inside and the tables outside, sometimes stopping long enough to see if anyone wanted anything more.

Momentarily, as I ate, my mind went back to my family? Are they eating this good? I thought to myself. I was greedy while I ate the food, but I was also feeling a twinge of guilt as I remembered my mother struggling to put enough food on the table to feed all of her kids and herself, too. It hurt too much to think on that so I pushed my fork into the potato salad and stuffed my mouth with it silencing the thoughts and forcing them to take another direction.

"I love having get-togethers like this with my church family," Bigmama said as she ran water in the kitchen sink to wash the last of the dirty dishes. The last of the guests had left and now the task of washing the dishes was at hand.

"Who cooked all of that food?!" L.C. asked, his eyes still wide from seeing so much food.

"All of the ladies from the church are responsible for the vegetables and the desserts. All of the men from the church are responsible for the meats and the drinks."

"How often do y'all do this," I wanted to know.

"Only once a year. Once a year we have an annual church outing and you know in the south every get-together, especially a church get-together, is planned around food—good food. Lots of good food!"

I nodded as if I understood what her comments meant. Of course I had no idea, but the food was delicious and for me that was all that mattered.

Bigmama immediately dumped the pots and pans into the hot soapy water and started to rub them clean with a white dishcloth.

"Can I help?" I asked Bigmama. I wanted to do all that I could to help her out and make her happy with L.C. and me.

She cocked her head to the side and looked at me with

a puzzled expression.

"You know how to wash dishes?" she asked backing away from the sink, drying her hands on the towel hanging from the door handle on the refrigerator.

"No, but I want to help you, Bigmama. You been cooking and waiting on everybody all day. Let me help you. Please," I told her.

"Come on. If you willing to try I'm willing to let you."

The water was hot to the touch of my hands. I searched around in the thick sudsy water until they touched one of the silver-colored pans.

"Lift it up out of the water," Bigmama instructed.

I did as she told me to do.

"Now you see that stuck on food at the bottom of it?" she asked looking at the side of my face.

"Yeah," I answered.

"Yeah?!"

"Yes, ma'am," I said rushing to correct the error I knew I had made once I had made it.

"Okay, that's better."

"Yes, ma'am. It is."

"Now wash around inside of there until all of that is completely gone. It's not clean until it has no trace of food on the inside or the outside."

"Yes, ma'am," I told her doing exactly as she had instructed me to do.

"Oh, no!" a familiar voice said entering the kitchen. It came from Jennetta. I wanted to disappear because I knew she would have something demeaning to say to me.

"Jennetta, don't come in here making fun," Bigmama said firmly.

"But Bigmama boys don't wash dishes," Jennetta responded sidling right up next to me.

I ignored her comments and scrubbed even harder the inside and the outside of the pans. Pleasing her was not my goal. My goal was to please Bigmama and learn how to do something I had never done before. Whether a boy was supposed to wash dishes or not was her opinion and she was indeed entitled to it just as I was.

"Get the broom and sweep, Jennetta," Bigdaddy ordered. He had entered the kitchen unnoticed.

Quickly, Jennetta crossed the short space from where she stood next to me to where the broom rested against the corner of the wall and began to do as Bigdaddy had instructed her to do. "And leave this here boy alone. I see you messing with him all the time."

From Persecution To Praise

"I'm just having fun with him, Bigdaddy. That's all!" Jennetta said back to her grandfather.

"Who you talking to like that?!" Bigdaddy asked in a high, tight tone. It sounded like he meant business to me.

"Sorry, granddaddy," she said sorrowfully.

"Now say sorry to Cedric," he ordered.

"Sorry, Cedric," she said sounding as if she meant it.

"It's okay," I told her keeping my eyes and mind on what I was doing—washing dishes. "I accept your apology."

As darkness fell, Bigmama and Bigdaddy ran our bath water and prepared us for bed. The house was quiet. Joyce and Jas were already ready for bed even though they were still watching television. Barbara had taken Jennetta home. I was glad of that. She was too much for me. She loved to make me look small. If she had been a boy I might have been tougher on her. She was a girl, and I was not supposed to hurt a girl. She acted like she hated me. Still, I began to think that she liked me more than she hated me.

Bigmama had turned the covers back for L.C. and me once we had our pajamas on.

"You know what we do before we go to bed. Right boys?" she asked looking first at L.C. then at me.

"Yes," we said together.

Immediately, we went down on our skinny knees and began to pray:

"Now I lay me down to sleep. I pray to the Lord my soul to keep. If I should die before I wake. I pray to the Lord my soul to take. Bless this house and everybody in it. Especially bless Bigmama and Bigdaddy. Bless our mama, brothers and sisters. Bless our daddy up in Heaven. Amen!"

Another Heart Break

Days turned into weeks. Weeks turned into months. Months turned into four years. It was the best four years of our lives. Bigmama taught me how to cook and clean house. She was a good cook, too. She kept a spotless house. The floors were so clean we could eat off of them if we had wanted to. We were expected to go to Sunday school and worship service every Sunday. We were expected to attend Wednesday night Bible class. Bigdaddy was a deacon at the church we attended and he was indeed faithful to his position and to his Lord.

Evenings were spent working in his small janitorial business. There I learned how to properly use cleaning agents to clean a building spotless. The vacuum cleaner was one of my favorite machines to clean with. I tried more than enough times to use the buffing machine.

However, my upper body lacked the strength to use it effectively. But I tried.

"Every man should know how to work," Bigdaddy said to me. "You will have a family one day and they will depend on you to take care of them. Working is an honorable man's duty."

Not only did I grow in stature, but I also grew in gifts and talents. I discovered I could actually draw. The news of my ability to draw beautiful, colorful scenes spread throughout my neighborhood as well as the city. Bigdaddy even mentioned my talent to the members of the board of alderman where he served in the district we lived in. Calls were coming from everywhere for me to draw a picture on mailboxes. It soon became a little business and I was able to make money from it.

"Boy, let nothing or no one stop you. No matter what your life looks like right now, God has a plan for you. You understand me boy?" Bigdaddy said to me.

I met his stare head on and opened my mouth to respond,

"Yes, Bigdaddy I understand."

"It ain't where your life starts," the older man went on. "It's where your life ends. I know you done had a rocky start. Losing your daddy at only three and your mama too is hard on anybody."

"Yes, it is," I whispered. He heard me speak though. He went on.

"But you ain't out of the game yet. You can be anything. You can do anything. As long as you put God first. The sky ain't even the limit. Trust in Him. No matter what happens to me and your Bigmama, stay with God."

Several months later Bigmama fell ill. Bigdaddy took her to the doctor and she was diagnosed with diabetes and high blood pressure. She was never the same after that diagnosis. Her footsteps slowed down along with her energy, but not before she gave L.C. and me one of the best Christmases of our lives.

Bigdaddy carried in huge chunks of wood and started a fire in the fireplace before putting a cookie sheet filled with chocolate chip cookie dough into the oven.

"Come on you two let's put up the Christmas tree," Bigmama told us.

We hung silver and gold ornaments all over it before wrapping it in glistening garland. When she pushed the plug into the wall outlet, the tree lit up with white lights. A gasped could be heard around the room.

"Turn off the lights," L.C. said with a big grin on his face.

Jas rushed to the light switched and turned it off. The wide eyes belonging to Bigdaddy, Bigmama, Joyce, Jas, L.C. and me glistened from the array of lights that filled the room. That Christmas L.C. and I were showered with gifts from new clothes, new shoes, new underwear, and new coats and new toys of every kind and variety. It had no reflection of the tragedy just up the road though.

Months later, Bigdaddy suddenly fell ill, too. He was very sick. I did not know what was wrong with him, but he stayed in the bed for days at a time. Bigmama was left to attend to him, Joyce, who was bedridden, L.C. and me and herself. It was wearing heavily on her and I could tell. The little energy she was operating with before now was cut even more. She was in bed as much, if not more, than Bigdaddy. Finally, after more days and weeks and months it was obvious they could no longer care for us. They called us to their bedside.

"Boys," Bigdaddy started, his breathing labored. "The time has come for your Bigmama and I to allow somebody else to love you too the way we have for the last four years."

From Persecution To Praise

Immediately, my heart started to race. Fear completely engulfed me.

"You mean. You mean," I stuttered. "You mean we got to leave you and Bigmama?"

"Yes, my babies," Bigmama said lying in the bed behind us. Bigdaddy and Bigmama slept in the same room, but not in the same bed. They had twin beds and L.C. and I stood between the two in shock. Bigmama went on.

"We just ain't able to care for you like we once did. Our bodies are sickly and our energy is low."

L.C. started to cry out loud. Bigdaddy got up from lying down, swung his aging legs over the side of his bed and reached for L.C.

"Come here," he said sympathetically. "Come to Bigdaddy."

Slowly, with his fingers in his mouth and tears streaming down either side of his face, he walked into Bigdaddy's outstretched hand. The older man pulled my little brother into a tight hug. "It's alright, my boy." His tone was not only sympathetic, but soothing as well.

"But it's not going to be alright!" I shouted out loud feeling wounded and disappointed and scared.

"Cedric!" Bigmama said sitting up in the bed. "You

must have faith that everything is going to be alright!"

"Faith! Faith!" I said now crying.

"Yes, the kind of faith in God that no matter what happens He is with you. How many times did I try to teach you that God loves you?"

"Love me?" I went on crying now harder. "If He loves me why do so many bad things happen to me and my brother? Why doesn't anyone want us?!"

"We can't answer that specifically, but all humans have a cross to bear, my child," Bigdaddy said stepping back into the conversation. "God has a plan for your life and L.C.'s. We don't know yet what it is, but you will understand it better, by and by."

"But it's not fair!" L.C. spoke between his tears.

"Life may not be fair. But God is. He loves you more than either of you can ever imagine. There are many issues in this ole life. We have to learn to deal with them the best that we can," Bigmama interjected.

"But it's so hard to deal with not being wanted!" I cried.

"You are wanted!" Bigmama reminded me.

"Then why are we leaving your house?! This is the best place we have ever been! Now we have to leave and go to a new house!"

"We do want you. Both of you," Bigdaddy said, stepping back into the conversation. "But it's our health. Our health is growing bad and the doctor has asked us to take it easy." Bigdaddy finished his thought and dropped his arms from around L.C. He lay back until the bed caught his body. He was still laboring to breathe.

"You all right over there?" Bigmama asked peering in Bigdaddy's direction.

He coughed in his fist then answered, "I'm okay. It's just I hate to have to send our boys away. That's all."

"Then don't do it!" I said rushing to Bigdaddy's bed side.

We met each other's stare the best we could. I could see tears forming in his milky eyes. I believed he was as hurt to see us have to go as we were hurt to have to go.

"Here," Bigmama said bringing a book from under her pillow and offering it to me. "Take this with you everywhere you go. This is your weapon and something to always remember me and your Bigdaddy. Read it every day and learn more about the love of God and His only begotten Son, Jesus. But just don't read it apply to your life what you read."

I took the book from her fingertips. It was the Holy Bible. A hush fell over the room as all eyes, including my own, fell on the black leather-bound book of life. An occasional sniffle could be heard along with the ticking of the clock on the wall as it ticked away the seconds, the minutes, then the hours. No one spoke. I was not sure if all the necessary words had been spoken or not, but I was all in my feelings trying to make sense out of what L.C. and I had just been told.

Back in our room, I climbed to the top bunk where I slept and L.C. followed close behind me.

"What now?" he asked.

I brought my shoulders up then down and answered him the best way I could to calm his fears. "No matter what happens to us now, we are going to be together. I promise never to leave you. I will always be here for you."

"You promise?" L.C. asked. I could see fear in his eyes that matched the same fear that I heard in his voice.

"Yes," I reassured him. "I will never let any hurt, harm or dangers come to you." Boy was I wrong.

MAMA J

The next home we were referred to by our social worker was a nightmare. How it started was not how it ended.

The day we left Bigmama and Bigdaddy Clemons was the worst day of my entire life—in a good way. The day we met our new foster mother was the worst day of my entire life—in a bad way.

"Welcome," our new foster mother said with a huge smile and a deep voice.

L.C. and I said nothing to her as we waved good-bye to Mr. Loftin, our social worker. Mrs. Jo was unavailable this time to accompany him with us.

"What do we call you?" L.C. asked our new foster mother once she closed the door to her home behind us.

"What do you want to call me?" the woman wanted to know.

L.C. looked at me and I looked at L.C. I believe he was waiting for my input. However, I was too absent-minded to have a thought that made any sense. So, I shrugged my shoulders to him.

"I tell you what," the woman said clasping her hands together, noticing the two of us struggling with what to call her. "Since my real name is Susie Mae Johnson. Just call me Mama J."

"Mama J," L.C. repeated using almost a hushed tone.

"Yes, Mama J is perfect," the dark-skinned, grey haired woman said. Her eyes widened as if she had found a miracle cure for a dreadful disease.

"Then Mama J it is," I opened my mouth to say not really caring at all. The ones I did care about, Bigmama and Bigdaddy, were now in my rearview mirror, and I knew I had to readjust to this seemingly nice woman.

Just then a little boy that appeared to me to be about eight or nine-years-old walked into the front room. Together our eyes shifted directly on him.

"Oh, by the way, this is your little brother, Dee, short for Denarious! Denarious is eight-years-old and has been with me about a year now! Denarious, say hello to your older brothers."

Even though L.C. nor I could understand the sound he made, we both returned a greeting, "Hello."

"Dee has some major physical challenges as you can see," the deep-voiced woman continued. "He wears diapers. He is unable to put words together and he can't bend his right arm. He's a good kid, and I believe you all will get along with him just fine. Right?"

Neither of us answered.

"Right?!" she asked again this time her tone high and tight.

"Yes, right," I said.

"Yes, right," L.C. agreed.

The small, slender-built boy covered the short space that separated each of us and wrapped his arms first around me and then around L.C. He then retraced his steps back to where he stood keeping his stare on us all the while.

"That's how he lets you know that he likes you," Mama J said proudly. "…by hugging you."

I completely ignored her excited chatter. My mind stayed on Bigmama and Bigdaddy. I just could not let my thoughts of them go. They had meant too much to me for so long. There was no one who could compare to the teaching and the love they had given to me and my brother while we lived in their home. The many times Bigmama allowed me into the kitchen to help her cook; the many times she took me fishing; the many times she told me she loved me and that everything was going to be alright; the many times she held me and comforted me when the tears would not stop flowing; the many times she took me to church and read to me the stories in the Bible and told me how much God loved me; the many times Bigdaddy showed me what it looked like to be a man with responsibilities; the many times he told me the importance of my education and always doing the right thing. Now they were no longer in our lives—taken away from us through sickness. I wanted to be angry. But who with?

"Cedric? Cedric, don't you hear me talking to you?!" Mama J snapped. She spit out the words as if they had a bad taste in her mouth.

I jumped—startled and scared—back into the moment.

"Where is your mind, boy?!" she wanted to know.

I told her the truth. "On Bigmama and Bigdaddy."

"Well Bigmama and Bigdaddy are out of the picture now. It's me and Dee and you and your little brother, L.C. Understand?"

"Yes, ma'am," I humbly answered.

"Now, that we are clear about that let me tell you how I run my house is probably nowhere near how Bigmama and Bigdaddy ran theirs. So, please, whatever you do don't ever let me hear either of you comparing the two homes. This is not Bigmama and Bigdaddy's home. It's mine. What I say goes. Period. Point blank."

Both L.C. and I looked at Mama J with wide-eyed suspicion and innocence. Neither of us knew what to make of what she had just shared. Still, the manner and tone in how she said it made us believe that she meant what she had said. Of course, we had no choice but to follow and obey. For now, this was the home that our social worker, Mr. Loftin, had placed us in.

"Let me show you your room. Follow me," the woman ordered, lifting both of her thin eyebrows to L.C. and me and walking away. We trailed her cautiously as she made her way in the direction of the hall.

"Right here is y'all's room," she said stopping just in front of the first door on the right. She reached her hand around the door facing and flipped on the light switch. The room lit up instantly. Our eyes scanned the room. The bedroom was spotless, but sparsely-furnished. The twin-sized beds were all that really mattered to L.C. and me, though. We had few clothes to put in the dresser drawers. The nightstand that rested between the two twin-sized beds had no use to us. I guessed it was there just in case someone visiting the room had use for it. It could of come as part of a bedroom suite—matching the headboards and the dresser.

Both beds had been layered with a multicolored bedspread. There was a colorful rag rug spread across the wood floor between the two beds. Cotton print curtains hung at the window which overlooked the back of the house.

"Okay, you two. I'm leaving it up to the two of you to decide which bed you will take," Mama J went on stepping into the middle of the room.

L.C. placed his suitcase on the one of the beds as a way of claiming it and I placed my suitcase on the other one not because it was my first choice, but because it was the choice that was left.

"The closet is over here."

Our eyes followed her to where she stood and pointed at a door on the south wall of the room. She swung the door open for us to see the empty space. One single hanger caught the wind of the door opening and began to swing back and forth.

"Now are there any questions?" she wanted to know.

"No," I answered.

L.C. simply shook his head.

The woman smiled a big smile and began to walk toward the door to exit the room. Just before entering into the hall she looked back at us. "Then I will give you two the time to settle in. I'll be in the kitchen preparing dinner. Make yourself at home. By the way, even though I did not show you, my bedroom is just down the hall, the last door to your right. If you should need me through the night, if I'm not working like tonight, that is where you will find me. Just be sure to knock and wait for me to say that you can come in."

The woman turned away from us and grabbed the hand of Dee who had stood silently at the door to the bedroom waiting for Mama J.

Dinner of meat, potatoes, and bread with red Kool-Aid was good. So was the hot bath. It was now time for bed. I waited for L.C. to turn back his own covers. We had been small boys when we first arrived at the Clemons' house and I remember I had folded back his covers and waited for him to climb in. However, since that time, we had grown quite a bit and it was time for L.C. to take on a bit more responsibility and turning back his own bed was a good place to start, I reasoned with myself.

"Remember what Bigmama and Bigdaddy taught us," I reminded L.C. Immediately, he remembered our bed time prayers. We both got down on our knees, next to our individual beds, bowed our heads, closed our eyes and prayed. When I got up from prayer L.C. was settling in between the clean white sheets spread across his mattress. I crossed the room, flipped the light switch and watched the room go very dark. I closed then opened my eyes a few times until they adjusted to the dark room before making my way back across the room to my bed. After tossing and turning and getting settled in, I called out L.C.'s name, but in a whispered tone. "L.C.!"

"What?" he answered back.

"What do you think of Mama J?" I wanted his opinion.

"I don't know. She seems nice."

"Yes, she does. But I can also tell she is not so nice, though."

"But how are you able to do that, Cedric?"

"I don't know. I can't explain it. I just feel it."

"What does it feel like?"

"It's a feeling that I've become too familiar with. She seems too nice."

"And?"

"And I just think there is more to her than what she is showing us."

"Well, we have to give her a chance. She might not be so bad."

"Yes, you are right, L.C. I guess Bigmama and Bigdaddy spoiled us. They were the best."

Yes, they were. But they are out of our lives now, Cedric."

What L.C. was saying to me, I should have been saying to him. After all, I was the oldest and probably should have more wisdom. Still, he was right—Bigmama and Bigdaddy were out of our lives and we had to trust somebody again—and Mama J just happened to be the one that was selected for the trust test.

"You're right, L.C." I started stepping back into the conversation after a brief few moments of silence. "I still miss Bigmama and Bigdaddy so much. I guess we have to move on continuing to wish for them is only going to keep me sad and I've been sad long enough."

"Me, too. So let's just give Mama J a chance. She might fool you."

"She might."

"We have no other choice right now." L.C. said. He finished with what he had to say and rolled over on his side, closed his eyes and drifted off to sleep. Me on the other hand, laid my head back until the cup of my clasped hands caught it. I stared at the ceiling rolling over and over in my head the good times we had at Bigmama's and Bigdaddy's.

"Why?" I spoke to the darkness. L.C. was sleep. I could hear the slight snoring sound coming from his nose. "Why did Bigmama and Bigdaddy have to get sick? Why couldn't they wait until we were grown and gone? Why another home?"

Of course I had no answers to my own questions and neither did the darkness that I was speaking to. We were stuck in another unfamiliar place with unfamiliar faces with no family to call on. I thought about my mother and the rest of my brothers and sisters. What were they doing right now? I wondered were they thinking of L.C. and me? Were they missing us the same way that we were missing them?

From Persecution To Praise

Finally, I gave up on the questions that I had no answer to. My eyelids were getting heavy as well, still I wanted to stay awake as long as possible unsure of the new woman and young boy who were living somewhere in the same house. I was L.C.'s big brother and what that meant to me was I was his protector and I did not want anything to happen to him in this new surroundings, and I was not able to protect him from it.

Just as a heavy dose of sleep nearly took me completely over, I heard voices and footsteps in the hall just outside of the door where L.C. and I slept. I heard the door to our room open then seconds later slam shut. I heard screaming. My heart began to pound while my eyes widened with fear. Mama J's wails burst through the walls along with an angry mumbled male voice.

I wanted to cover my head with the pillow, and yet I wanted to hear whatever I could. So, I raised my head a bit. I figured that since it was dark in the room seeing my wide eyes would be next to impossible. I lay still and waited to see what was going to happen next. Once again the door to the room we slept in opened and slammed shut. I heard a set of footsteps hurry down the hall. I waited, desperate to know what was happening and yet too fearful to find out what it was. Two weeks later, I found out.

A Taste For Blood

Mama J worked night shift at a local manufacturing plant. She readied herself while we waited for the babysitter to arrive.

"Make sure you all keep the house clean. Do your homework, and get in kindling and firewood for the fireplace. It's supposed to get colder tonight. No company over at all," Mama J advised before walking out of the house and into the evening. It was early October. The very warm weather had now been swept completely away by a sudden chill from a north wind.

"Come on you guys, it's time to do your homework," Kim the babysitter told us emphatically. This time she was not playing. The evening was far spent. Our day at school was over and she had allowed us to play with our video games for most of the evening.

"Just let us finish this game," I begged as my thumbs worked as fast as I could get them to.

Kim stood with her arms folded over her chest and patted impatiently her left foot waiting.

"Okay," I finally said to her before turning to L.C. and saying, "We'll finish this when we get done with our homework."

"No, you won't," Kim said.

I looked up at her and asked, "Why not?"

"Because then you have to get the firewood in like Mama J told you to do."

Kim was a great babysitter. She allowed us to do nearly what we wanted to do as long as we did not destroy the house and did our homework. She loved to play video games with us and sometimes brought CD's for us to dance to. When it came to rules, she insisted that we obey Mama J. We pulled out books and paper from our bookbags that had been resting in the closet, and sat down at the kitchen table to begin doing our homework. Kim helped us out whenever we had a problem that we did not understand. Soon, we were finished.

"Can we finish that game now?" L.C. wanted to know. "Please?"

Kim threw her eyes up at the ceiling then brought them back down and put them on L.C. first then on me. She thought for a moment then looked at her watch.

"Okay, it's just about seven o'clock. We all know that Mama J gets off work at eleven. The firewood is still outside which means it's not inside, and you two are responsible for making that happen. So, I'm going to give you twenty minutes to finish that game, and you have to finish your chores, period. Got that?" she finished matter-of-factly.

"Yes," L.C. and I said at the same time.

Kim pivoted on the heels of her red sneakers and left the room. Immediately, our thumbs got busy working fiercely to beat the other at the game.

That all ended when we heard the front door open. "Mama J is home!" I exclaimed after hearing the front door close. "We haven't gotten in the firewood!"

Fear suddenly gripped L.C. and me. Quickly, we disconnected the game and hurried toward the bedroom door and threw it open. It was not Mama J, instead a big hulking man we had never seen before stood staring angrily down at us.

We gasped at the sight of him. The skin on his face

was tight and shiny. The muscles in his arms were thick and huge like he had been working out for years. He opened his mouth and started in on the both of us.

"So, playing games before getting in firewood?!" he asked hypothetically with an unexplained rage.

"But I told them they had time," Kim rushed to say standing behind him, in an attempt to defend us. His body was so wide that we couldn't even see her.

"No, they don't have time!" he barked directing his voice over his left thick shoulder towards Kim.

It was the same voice I remembered hearing on the night we moved in a few weeks ago. He was arguing with Mama J. I was not sure if the big man towering over us was Mama J's brother or boyfriend. That confusion was cleared up the minute he walked away and disappeared down the hall into Mama J's bedroom.

"That's Mama J's boyfriend, Lee," Kim told us, her breathing a bit more heavy. "And he is meaner than a junkyard dog. Trust me."

"We do. So we better get going so that we don't make the junkyard dog madder," I responded with wisdom I did not know I had.

Quickly, L.C. and I swung open our closet door and

pulled out warm clothes. We slipped them on just as fast and went out the back door into the dark, cold night to get firewood.

Shivers ran up and down my arms then suddenly all over my body. We made our way to the wood that was stacked several feet high under the carport.

"Here," I told L.C. who had both of his arms extended, "Take these." One by one I loaded four or five small round logs onto his arms then opened the back door for him to carry them into the house.

"Stack them over there, boy," Lee ordered out of nowhere. L.C. stared directly at him bringing his thick eyebrows together in a frown. L.C. shifted his eyes to avoid his gaze.

"You rolling your eyes at me, boy?!" Lee snapped at L.C.

"No, sir," L.C. said quickly, growing afraid and backing away from the big man's space.

"Then get a move on. When I tell you to do something, don't let grass grow under your feet! Be quick about it!" he yelled continuing to come towards L.C. aggressively. L.C., frightened, continued to back up.

My heart was beating so hard I could hear it pounding

in my ears. I was scared to death but managed to stammer, "Leave my brother alone!"

Lee seemed to be deaf to what I said to him. His evil eyes were stuck on my little brother's face. He backed L.C. into a corner. There was no place left for my brother to go. In one effortless motion he snatched L.C. up by the wrist and pulled him toward himself. Lee reached for a piece of kindling with his free hand. The kindling was conveniently lying next to the firewood we had just stacked, but Lee didn't use it to start a fire. He used it to beat my brother. He beat him and beat him, and kept on beating him.

"Please stop hitting my brother!" I cried out loud. "Please!"

Over and over and over again the man hit L.C. with the splintered kindling. L.C. cried out, "What did I do?! Why?!"

The licks soon tore into my brother's flesh, and blood started to flow from them. The blood triggered something in me. It enraged me to the point I had to do something before he beat my brother to death. I jumped on Lee's back. I was like a gnat on the back of an elephant. He shook me off so hard that I landed next to the couch bumping my head hard against the corner of it.

"Oh, Lord!" I cried out grabbing the side of my head. My plea to God must have work, just as fast as my brother's beating started it was over. Lee walked hard across the floor as he left passing by me without even looking down. Across the room, my brother, L.C. lay in a fetal position whimpering like the wounded child he was. Slowly, I pulled myself across the floor to where he lay sobbing uncontrollably. I draped an arm around his shoulders, and we lay there together crying hard and alone.

Kim was nowhere to be found. Apparently she had run away from the chaos once it got started. After a while, slowly and quietly, I managed to pull myself up from the floor with L.C. holding on to me.

In our room, behind the closed doors, I used a warm, wet towel and attended to his wounds. His skin was broken and oozing blood on his arms, legs, and even his face. Wrapping my arms around him, I tried to create a place of comfort for him to rest.

Terrified, I held his warm, shivering body through the storm of his wails and sobs before lifting the hem of my pajama top and drying his tears. I stroked his head and soothed him until he fell asleep. But I, on the other hand, lay awake long after, until the sky was streaked with brightness. Overnight, my baby brother's uncontrollable tears had settled into a lump of bitterness in the pit of my stomach. Automatically I knew things for me would never be the same. I was no longer a little boy. What had just happened to L.C. forced me into a place of adult responsibility with an unfriendly world and there was no turning back. From that day forward I had a taste for blood. I would wreak havoc on whoever provoked me. This would become a problem for me in the days and years to follow especially at school. The rage had set in deep and only the spirit of God could remove it now.

Lord Help Us

The very next morning before the start of the first period class, Mama J and I met with Mr. Garth, the middle school principal, who was sitting grim-faced at his desk. I knew by the tightness around his jawline that the trouble I was in was big. However, the severity of the punishment was what I did not know. Expelled? Suspended? Transferred to another school district?

"Good morning, Miss. Johnson, Cedric," Mr. Garth greeted, a cold edge to his voice. He took a sip of water from his stainless-steel tumbler and turned to me. "Derrick has told me his side of the story. What is yours?"

"Hodges started with me first," I mumbled. "It wasn't my fault."

"Of course, that's what Hodges said. Mr. Doss, I

propose you tell me what really happened," Mr. Garth said, his voice thick with contempt. "Most of the students at this school tell me that you have a bad attitude and will fight at the drop of a dime. These allegations are serious. It's time for you to share what's been going on with you causing such behavior as yours."

"Tell the truth, Cedric," Miss. Johnson pressed. How dare she.

"What y'all heard were lies. Nothing but lies. I never hurt nobody. I'm the one who always gets bullied. Since I'm the new kid here the blame will always fall on me. You just don't know..." I started then stopped talking and threw my eyes up then brought them down.

"Just don't know what?" Mr. Garth asked leaning forward.

"I get tired of being laughed at, talked about. I ain't got no mama, no daddy, people calling me foster boy." Even though I could feel the hot tears threatening to come, I bit down hard on my bottom lip immediately stopping the flow.

"Go on," the principal insisted.

"They think just because I'm little they can take me. What they say about me hurts. So when they hurt me, I hurt them back. It's just that simple."

"Listen, Mr. Doss," Mr. Garth started in an angry pitch. "You are very close to being sent home maybe for the rest of the year. Do you understand the words that are coming from my mouth?"

"They think I'm a loser. A psycho. Homeless." I rebutted.

"There is nothing I can do about the name calling." Mr. Garth started up after I finished. "You are going to have to put your big boy pants on and let this stuff roll off your back or you will be fighting every day, all day. You have an education to fight for. Put your energy into that. You know who you are."

"I'm just desperate for it all to end." I said as I lowered my head in my hands—humiliated. I felt my face grow hot with shame as I struggled to maintain a hint of pride. The sadness inside of my soul seemed to overwhelm all of me—mind, body, and spirit.

"He seems to think the whole school hates him," Miss. Johnson added, after sitting quiet throughout the entire conference. It was as if her boyfriend wasn't an huge issue also.

Cedric cut an evil eye at her and added, "And I think

you hate me, too." Surprised by my open confession, I believe a lump rose up in Mama J's throat so thick that she was not able to come back with a response.

Principal Garth raised his eyebrows to both of us before adding, "Look, I think you two should go home and talk things over. I believe there are some problems and they must be handled at home. In the meantime, Mr. Doss, I have to expel you for five days for fighting. Hopefully, during this time you can settle whatever it is that's going on and come back with a different attitude and perspective. If you don't, I will be left with no other alternative, but to send you home for the rest of this year."

"You ain't nothing but a punk!" Lee, Mama J's boyfriend, screamed later that evening after finding out I had been expelled from school for fighting. "And you dumb!"

Lee grabbed hold of my shirt collar with both of his thick hands, lifting me up from the floor high enough for our faces to meet within inches of each other. "What you got to say now bad boy?" He growled.

I shrugged my shoulders sternly meeting Lee's gaze as best I could. He then dropped both of his thick hands from my shirt collar and let me hit the floor. I lay there waiting his next move.

"Get up and fight me like you fight at school!" Lee pressed, reaching down and picking me up from the floor and standing me on my feet. I fell back to the floor, my legs feeling too weak to stand on.

"Look at me boy when I'm talking to you!"

The older man reached down and brought my face up by my chin. I refused to meet his gaze this time. I had given up the will to push back. Rather, I just wanted the big man to punish me and get it over with. That he did. Again, his huge thick hands grabbed my shirt collar. He swept me up from the floor and began to shake me violently. I refused to fight back. There was no need. I knew it was next to impossible for me to win. So, he continued to beat me. He shakes me so violently that my head spun into a throbbing headache, after which he threw me into the side of the refrigerator causing it to rock.

"You think you bad?! I'll show who's bad!" With this Lee balled his fist and slammed it into my face splitting my lip. The blood splattered the wall, the refrigerator, and the front of my shirt. I cringed trying to brace for the next blow.

"I'm sorry! I'm sorry!" I finally screamed as the taste

of blood filled my mouth, and I covered my face with both of my hands. He eyed me spitefully and left the house with Mama J. She had witnessed the entire beating and had said nothing nor interfered to keep me from being abused by her man.

Slowly, I got up and drug myself down the hall and into my room. I went to the closet and opened it. The closet door had a mirror on it and the face I saw reflecting in it scared me. My face was swollen. My lips were twice their normal size. A blue and purple color ring circled my right eye.

"Oh, my goodness!" I gasped. I looked older than twelve. In fact, my face was so distorted I could not tell how old I looked. I sighed in disbelief, just then I noticed the reflection of my little brother L.C. His eyes said the same thing I felt. He stood behind me in horror. His book bag hit the wood floor with a loud thud as he rushed to my side draping his arm across my shoulders.

"What happened to your face!?" he asked with wide eyes. I shook my head first in disbelief and disgust. I didn't want to repeat what had just happen, but I knew he had to know. My head ached still and my mouth was swollen but I managed to finally says that Lee had beaten me.

"What?! Why?!"

"I got into another fight at school today, and Principal Garth expelled me for five days. Mama J of course told him and he..he.." The rest of the words caught in my throat along with the feeling of helplessness that rushed to the surface.

"I hate that man," L.C. said, slamming his curled fist into his hand and gritting his teeth. "I hate this house!" he spoke in haste. Neither of us knew Mama J was listening. She had been listening the entire time.

"Well get out! Noooow!" she said in a voice that sounded almost demonic.

Both L.C. and I jerked our heads in her direction. She stood before us with the most evil look in her eyes that we had ever seen on any person. Our eyes followed her outstretched arms down to the boney wrinkled finger that pointed to the back door. She could not be serious, but she was. We considered and reconsidered her demand. "But it's cold out there!" L.C. pleaded.

"You should've thought about that before you decided to speak what you just spoke! If you hate this house and don't want to be here, get the hell out! Nooow!" She held the word now yet again just not as long this time.

We believed she was very serious. My brother and I exchanged looks and started towards the direction of the door. Mama J. walked ahead of us. Once we got there, she placed her foot in our path. "Go back!" she demanded. We both released a heavy sigh, but drew in a deep breath as she finished with her thought. "Undress."

"What?!" I asked, bringing my eyebrows together in confusion.

"Those clothes that you are wearing, I bought. Since you hate this house that means you hate me. If you hate me then that means you hate my money. It was my money that bought them. So strip!"

We could not believe our ears. A feeling of bewilderment and disbelief over shadowed us. I felt hopeless, but something inside me took me back to Bigmama's house. I summoned some much needed courage, remembering Bigmama's teachings that God would never leave us or forsake us. Suddenly, I felt a hint of peace wash over me; however, it was quickly dissolved once the thirty degree night air hit our naked bodies.

"It's cold out here," L.C. said his lips quivering along with his thin body.

I was cold as well. I knew I had to be strong for L.C. and take care of him. So, I looked around for a place for us to huddle together under the carport—a place where the brutal wind could not find us. Still, the night was cold as we wrapped ourselves up in the arms of the other and looked up to the starry night sky hoping to catch a glimpse of the God Bigmama and Bigdaddy taught us about.

Never forget to pray, I remembered Bigdaddy telling me during our talks. So, I looked at L.C. and said," Let's pray."

"Go ahead," he told me feeling too cold to even open his mouth or part his lips.

"Lord, help us," I prayed. They were the only three words I could get out.

Cedric Doss

A Call For Help

Mama J's attitude toward L.C. and me grew worse as time went on. For a day or two she was the greatest person alive to us. For the next day or two she was the worst person alive to us. When she was not hitting us or throwing things at us, it was her boyfriend, Lee. Even when she was mad at him, she took it out on us, sending us out into the cold night without clothes on our young backs.

We never knew how she was going to react to any situation at any given time. This kind of behavior kept us fearful and on our toes—hating her and Lee more and more.

Kim, our babysitter, helped us to recognize those things that triggered bad behavior in her—causing her to mistreat us. Over time, it seemed to us that even our best behavior was not enough to keep her from going off on us.

She was like a keg of dynamite. I desperately needed to speak to someone about her increasingly hateful behavior toward L.C. and me. The abuse between her and her boyfriend, Lee, had gotten unbearable.

"I'm going to write a letter to Mr. Loftin, our social worker," I whispered to L.C. one night after going to bed.

"Do you have his address?" L.C. wanted to know.

"No, but I will ask Kim to get it for me."

"Wait a minute," L.C. started, remembering something.

"What?! What?!" I wanted to know after noticing L.C. thinking on something.

"Remember when Mrs. Jo brought us to Bigmama and Bigdaddy's house?"

"Yes," I answered sitting up in my bed and throwing my eyes over at L.C. "What about it?"

"She gave you a piece of paper with her number on it and told you to call her if we ever needed her. Remember that?"

I nodded yes thinking back to that time. "But what did I do with it?"

L.C. shrugged his shoulders then answered, "I don't know. Check in your suitcase."

L.C. then threw his legs over the side of his bed and we

both rushed to the closet. The black average-sized suitcase belonging to me rested against the wall in the back of the closet. I reached for it like it was a prized possession. It was the golden ticket to the answer to our sick and disgusting dilemma. Needing to contact the social worker was an understatement. We were going to die if we did nothing.

"Boys, is anything wrong?" Kim asked, cracking the door and throwing her voice through it.

"No," I answered.

"Then what are you two doing out of bed and in the closet?" Kim asked, opening the door wider.

"We're looking for a piece of the video game we misplaced," L.C. lied.

"In the dark? Why not flip on the light?"

Just then the room was flooded with light. She had turned it on while she spoke to us. L.C. and I caught Kim's gaze.

"Oh, my goodness, Cedric! What happened to your face?!" Kim asked, her eyes wide with horror. She rushed across the space and dropped to her knees alongside me.

"Lee beat me again." I honestly told her, dropping my gaze feeling ashamed of how I looked.

Kim reached out and gently touched my face. I recoiled.

"Does it hurt?" she asked, appearing genuinely worried.

"Yes."

"It looks like it does. That is awful. We have to do something about that. He shouldn't get away with treating you like that way. He could've killed you."

I figured Kim had shown enough genuine concern for my injuries to share with her why we were really in the closet.

"I want to call my social worker and report this," I told her.

"Do you have the number?" Kim asked.

"That's what we're looking for now," I told her never looking at her directly.

"Yes, I lied," L.C. said, speaking up immediately.

"But I thought you guys trusted me. You don't have to lie to me. Seriously, this needs to be reported."

"We weren't for sure that we could," I said to her.

"So, where in this closet are you two looking for a telephone number to your social worker?" Kim went on her eyes scanning the small space.

"We're not exactly sure, but I think it might be in my

suitcase," I said.

The young lady laid her eyes on the suitcase that was still resting against the wall of the closet. She reached out and grabbed the handle dragging it right up to where she sat on her knees. She dragged the zipper around the entire suitcase and laid back the top of it.

"There's nothing here that I can see," she told us.

Neither of us could see anything that looked like a slip of paper. However, I pointed to the compartment attached to the top of the suitcase.

"Look in there," I suggested praying at the same time.

Kim followed my orders. She fished inside of the compartment. When she pulled her hand out in it was the envelope with Mrs. Jo's information on it.

"You looking for this?!" she asked, holding it up and looking at me.

I blew a heavy sigh of relief and said, "Yes! That's it!"

"So, when do you plan to call your social worker?" Kim asked, releasing the slip of paper into my hand before standing to her feet.

"Tomorrow," I answered without even thinking about it.

"Tomorrow? You're in school tomorrow," Kim said

looking confused.

"No, I'm not," I told her.

"What do you mean?" she pressed. "It's a holiday?"

"No. I'm expelled."

"Expelled?!" she exclaimed surprised. "For what?!"

"For fighting."

"Fighting? Fighting with who?"

"This guy named Hodges. He's been picking on me for a long time. Since I've been at that school actually. He's not the only one. Lots of the kids meddle and make fun of me. Calling me orphan boy. Saying I ain't got no mama or daddy."

Kim stood silent as I shared with her my situation at school. When I finished sharing, she asked, "So, how much of this did Hodges do?"

"None of it. I got the best of him. In fact, I was so angry I hit him over and over again until blood flew from his nose."

"Then what?" Kim pushed.

"That woman…" I started up and was interrupted by Kim.

"You mean, Mama J? What did she do?"

"She brought me home and shared me being expelled

with Lee and then he just started hitting me."

"Wow!" Kim said.

"Yes, that's about it."

"That's enough. But I understand why you want to leave. I would want to leave, too, if I got a beating like he put on you. Tomorrow will be a good time to call your social worker. Do it while she is asleep. Right now you two need to sleep. So, get to bed. In the morning, when you think she is in a deep sleep, go for it. If there is anything that I can do just ask. I know you have suffered a bunch living here with Mama J and Lee. I think she is crazy."

"Yes, we've been thinking the same thing."

Kim turned to leave. I called out after her. "Thank you, Kim."

"For what?"

"For being our friend," I said getting up from down. "You have been so kind to us. Without you I don't know what we would have done. I'm sorry that a nice person like you has to work for someone that has such a bad attitude."

"Well, not for long," Kim told me, stopping just before exiting the room.

"You quitting?" L.C. said, finally standing to his feet

and walking in her direction.

"Actually, I'm moving into a college dorm on campus where I go to school at. I had been commuting back and forth, but a room has become available and I'm moving into it in a few days."

" Great! Good luck and may God bless you!" I told her joining her and L.C. at the door.

"Thank you. May God bless you two as well. Things will get better. Just keep the faith. I love you boys. "Now get in the bed." Kim corralled them into a big hug and stepped into the hall closing the door behind her.

The next morning, L.C. climbed out of bed, got his breakfast and met the bus all on time. I, on the other hand, lay in bed listening to the sound of the bus as it pulled off from the front of our house and made its way through the neighborhood.

"I hope you don't think these five days will mean you're on vacation," Mama J said, throwing open the door and stepping inside the room.

Quickly, I sat up in bed unsure of what she was going to do next.

"Now get your lazy behind out of that bed and get in there and scrubbed that kitchen floor. When you finish scrubbing that floor get to the hall bathroom and scrub that toilet. Then come to my room and scrub the toilet in there. Please don't make a lot of noise because I done worked all night and I want to get some sleep. Got that?"

"Yes, ma'am," I quickly answered, rushing to get out of bed.

By the time I finished with scrubbing the kitchen floor and scrubbing the toilet in the hall bathroom, I carried my bucket and sponge down the hall in the direction of Mama J's bedroom. Just before entering I could hear her snoring. This led me to believe she was in a deep sleep. I remembered what Kim had expressed to me the night before, do it while she is asleep. Not only did I believe the older woman was sleep, but she was in a deep sleep. I stood outside of the door for a few more minutes thinking about the envelope in my pocket and how soon should I make the call. Now is a good time, I thought to himself. Then I walked softly back down the hall and into the kitchen, setting the bucket gently down on the floor and placing the sponge on the countertop.

Slowly, I reached inside of my front pants pocket and pulled out the envelope and the paper inside and unfolded it. Clearly, Mrs. Jo's seven-digits were on it. Looking around the area, I noticed the phone resting on the desk in the kitchen. I crept over to it and stared down at the phone for a few seconds before slowly picking it up. I called the number and waited for someone to answer.

"County Department of Human Services, how may I direct your call?" a lady's voice said. I was paralyzed in my thoughts. Even my lips would not move.

"Hello," the lady's voice said again. "Is anyone there?"

"Yes, me."

"Me? How may I direct your call?"

"I would like to speak to Mr. Loftin, please," I finally said after my lips decided to move.

"I'm sorry, but Mr. Loftin is not in the office at this time. May I take a message?"

All of the air went out of my sail. I was too afraid to leave Mama J's number. She would know I had tried to contact my social worker and that would be problematic for me.

"Ahhh, no. No message. I'll call back. Thank you." I hung up the phone and stood in place for more than a few seconds feeling completely defeated.

"So, you want to talk to your social worker, huh?" Mama J asked. She had entered the kitchen and I had not even noticed. "What did you have to tell him?"

Mama J walked toward me. I started backing up tripping over the bucket of water I had placed on the floor. The water sprayed all over the laminate flooring. Mama J did not even mind it. Her gaze was totally focused on me and mine was totally focused on her. Fear gripped me. I just knew she was going to kill me. Quickly, I got up from falling over the bucket slipping and sliding in an attempt to get away from her.

Crack!

Mama J had grabbed a stick of wood from resting alongside the fireplace and hit me over the back of my head. The sound the lick made rocketed through my skull sending me sprawling backwards into the garbage can. Smelly garbage landed all over me including my face.

For several long minutes I lay motionless as the pain went up and down the back of my head. Only until I managed to sit up could I grab that spot. Immediately, my hands felt the thick, hot blood oozing from the open wound. Alarmed by the amount of blood on my hand, I struggled to get to my feet. My vision became blurry and I seemed to be drifting into unconsciousness, believing too, that getting to my feet would be impossible. I knew I had to in order to save my life. My head throbbed mightily, and I had to grab a hold of the edge of the countertop to keep from falling back into the garbage can once more.

Mama J dropped the stick of wood, pivoted on the heels of her bare feet, went back down the hall and climbed into bed as if she did not have an emergency on her hand.

I staggered next door. The neighbors not only attended to my wounds, but also comforted me before calling Mr. Loftin.

Facing Momma

William and Annie Henderson welcomed both L.C. and me into their lovely home with no hesitation. They seemed to love us and wanted to make a happy, wholesome home. They wanted us to receive a good education. It was important to Mr. and Mrs. Henderson. So, they quickly enrolled us into public school. However, upon my arrival, I was met with some bitter-sweet news.

"Cedric!" a young female voice called out to me after getting off the bus in front of the school.

I turned around to meet the big, brown eyes belonging to a brown-skinned girl with a gap between her two front teeth. I brought my eyebrows together in confusion.

"Hi!" she said joyfully. "My name is Lola! I'm your cousin!"

For the first time in years I had met someone sharing my DNA. I did not know whether to be happy or concerned.

"Hi," I finally said guardedly, staring back at the young girl.

"So, you are going to this school now?!" she went on starting to walk alongside me as I moved away from her.

"Yes." I answered and nodded at the same time. "Yes, I'm going to this school now."

"It's been a long time since I've seen you," Lola went on. "When we were like very little kids."

"Yes, it has been a long time. We were kids."

I did not know exactly what to say to her, but what she said was at least interesting to me. I wanted to continue the conversation.

"Do you live around here?" I wanted to know. I figured if I found out where she lived that might lead me to my mother and siblings.

"Yes, just a few streets over. Where do you live now?" she asked.

"I live on Davidson County Line."

"Where is that?"

"Way over there somewhere. I'm not sure."

"Oh, okay."

Just then the bell rang interrupting our conversation.

"Got to run," the girl said rushing off. "I'll see you at recess!"

"Bye," I said waving to her back.

The halls were bustling with kids opening and closing lockers—rushing to get to class on time. I was in no hurry.

Seemingly, I could not get the girl, Lola, who claimed to be my cousin, off my mind. As I walked the halls thinking over what had just been shared with me and looking for Room 312, I pulled a piece of candy from my pocket, twisted open the wrapper and popped the green apple-tasting treat into my waiting mouth.

"Hey, boy!" a lady I did not know shouted out to me. She was resting against a broom and had an evil look in her eyes while staring at me. "Come back here right now and pick that paper up you just dropped on my clean floor!"

My heart quickly started to race. A hint of fear rose up in my chest.

"Yes..Yes, ma'am," I answered stuttering. Of course I wasted no time doing what the woman said. I reached down and picked up the piece of paper. I didn't even know I had dropped it.

"Now, get your butt to class and stop slow poking around. As long as you at this school I better never, ever see you drop a piece of paper on this floor again. You got that?!"

"Yes, ma'am." I said hurrying to class.

The next morning when I exited the bus, my cousin Lola, was waiting for me just inside of the fence in front of the school building.

"Hey, cuz!" she rushed to me with a big gap-toothed smile. "How you doing?!"

"I'm okay," I answered letting my guard down a bit.

"Come with me. I have someone I want you to meet!"

"Who is it?" I wanted to know, suddenly feeling a bit suspicious.

"Just come on," she insisted reaching out her hand and taking mine pulling me with her.

She pulled me all the way across the school yard until we reached a woman with her back turned to us.

"Miss. Louberta," the girl started.

The woman who had gotten onto me just the day before about dropping paper on her very clean floor turned around to face us. The same feeling of fear quickly rushed through my body, yet again. I drew in a deep breath and stood nervously staring at the woman.

"Yes," she answered. "What you want with me?"

"Here, meet your son, Cedric. Cedric, meet your mom, Louberta."

My heart dropped, along with my bottom lip. The woman's eyes got as big as a quarter as we both stood staring at the other in complete shock.

"Hi, my son," the woman started. "I've missed you so much. I've always wondered where you were."

She reached out and brought my hand into a tight squeeze. It seems my head automatically rested in her chest. Immediately, though, I withdrew, resisting her attempt at showing me her affection. I stiffened against her touch refusing to bring my arms around her.

"Aren't you going to hug your mother back?" Lola wanted to know. "She's your mother, Cedric."

I did not acknowledge either of them. When the woman dropped her arms from around me, I quickly pivoted on the heels of my sneakers and rushed into the school building.

The next day when I exited the bus, Lola was not there to greet me as she had done in the days past. My mother, Louberta was standing there, however, waiting for me.

"Cedric!" she called out.

Even though I heard her, I ignored her and continued to walk hurriedly in the direction of the school building. Soon she caught up with me and handed me a brown paper bag.

"Here, I brought you something," she told me. I stopped moving forward long enough to open the bag and peer inside of it. Candy, oranges, and apples was what my eyes fell on. Immediately, I closed the bag up and threw it at my mother's head and angrily scowled her, "I don't want it! I don't want anything from you, ever! Leave me alone and never speak to me again! You left me with strangers!"

"But I loved you. I wanted to keep you, but I couldn't. It was too hard after your father was killed."

"I don't care how hard it was no mother ever gives up her child! Get away from me! I hate you!"

A Downward Spiral

Soon thereafter my life started to unravel. My mother did not recognize me nor I her. How does that happen? I was so angry all the time. I felt hopeless and alone. I cared about nothing and no one. This made it easy to get into trouble everywhere even the neighborhood I lived in.

"Are you kidding me?" Mrs. Henderson began. "You broke in my mother's house and stole her money? She's an old lady. Why did you do that, Cedric?"

I stood next to the chair where Mrs. Henderson sat questioning me. Mr. Henderson was sitting on the couch resting across the space where the chair sat holding Mrs. Henderson.

"Cedric," the older man's voice started. "Answer my wife. Now! Why did you break into that house?!"

I humped my shoulders up and down before replying with a nonchalant "I don't know."

"That's not the truth, Cedric and you know it," the soft spoken woman said to me shaking her head at the same time. "We all know why we do what we do. I know it wasn't because you needed money. You don't have anything you need to buy. We take care of you. Good care of you."

Mr. Henderson stepped back into the conversation summarizing his disappointment, "So, while you were there to buy snacks, you and all of your friends, your clique, you decided to slip and unlock a window behind my mother-in-law's back only to come back later to steal? Wow!"

A sudden silence crept into the room. I know they were sitting there trying to understand my blatant disrespect. It was deeper than they could decipher. It was deeper than the love they showed me had the capacity to cover.

"Now, we wanted to help you," Mrs. Henderson started, stepping back into the conversation. "And we still want to help you. But we won't tolerate criminal behavior while you live here with us. If you choose the behavior, you have to accept the consequences."

"The consequences of stealing and other criminal

activity are going to lead you and that little group of yours straight to juvenile hall." Mr. Henderson added. The talk Mr. and Mrs. Henderson had with me apparently was not serious enough, because within days, I sneaked out of the house at two in the morning, rounded up my buddies and went bike stealing in the neighborhood miles from our own only to be caught again.

"Hey, you!" an angry male voice shouted out threateningly. "Come back with my child's bike!"

My friends and I were caught red-handed stealing bikes. The homeowner carried me straight back to my foster parent's house and knocked on the door.

"Mr. Henderson," the unknown man stated after Mr. Henderson opened the door.

"Yes," Mr. Henderson answered tying and retying his robe.

"I'm bringing your son home."

"Huh?" Mr. Henderson said unbelievingly. "It's three in the morning."

"Yes, I know. I surprised him and his buddies. They were stealing bikes over in my neighborhood and thought everybody was sleep. I heard the noise in my backyard and came out of my house to find Cedric sneaking off with my child's bike. I ain't going to press no charges against him because I know you and y'all good people. I got my child's bike back."

"Thanks," Mr. Henderson said looking at the man. He then turned his gaze on me. I had to drop my stare. It was too hard to look him knowing he and his wife had only done good by me. "Now you get your butt in this house! Right now!" he demanded. Mr. Henderson was very angry.

Just before the man turned to step off the porch, he said matter-of-factly, "The next time I catch him trying to take something from my property, I'm going to get the police involved before somebody kill him."

Within the next few days, I was back at my criminal behavior. I broke into another house in the neighborhood and stole a gun and money. My friend told on me, and I was sent to juvenile hall.

"We told you," Mr. and Mrs. Henderson said. "When you do the crime, Cedric, you must do the time. We tried, but you were hardheaded. So, now you have to suffer the consequences. By the way you no longer have a room in our home. You are too much trouble, and you're only sixteen. I don't want to even think about what you will like at seventeen or eighteen. We love you. L.C. can stay, but you got to go. Good-bye, Cedric."

Cedric Doss

Locked Up

I came full circle. I was returned to the Mississippi Home for Children in Jackson, Mississippi where I had left to go live with the Clemons many years earlier. However, I did not stay long before a relative of the Henderson's reached out to bring me home with him. The monster inside of me crept back into my thoughts enticing me to go back to my old ways and old habits—breaking in houses and stealing guns and money.

"You're nothing but trouble!" the elderly gentleman scowled. "You done even broke in my house! You don't do nothing but sit around this house and play Tupac music all day! That's why your mind all misguided! You got to go!"

Back to Jackson, Mississippi to the Mississippi Home

for Children I went. This time I was more bitter and angrier than ever before. Still, the stay did not last very long. I was given yet another chance. The Henderson's son reached out to me and brought me home with him.

"Listen, man," the young Henderson said. "I want to help you, but you got to want to be helped. You have been given chance after chance. You blew them. Don't blow this one. I will do everything in my power to see you get on your feet and live a decent life, but the stealing and breaking in people's houses got to go. If not, you're either going to jail or to the graveyard. The choice is yours. Now, I work at night and you will have to kind of govern yourself. You have a home here as long as you stay out of trouble. You got that?"

"Yes, I got that," I responded.

Yes, I did get it, but I thirsted for stealing. In the trailer park, where the young Henderson lived, trailers were empty for most of the day—people were at work. I did not spend my days in school because I was in eighth grade at sixteen. So, stealing became my daily routine.

There was a vacant trailer where I stored my spoils. Each day, I broke into one of the occupied trailers and stole until one day I came face-to-face with the landlord.

"If I catch you breaking into one more trailer I'm going to kill you!" the man said between gritted teeth.

I ran my wide eyes down the long-barreled rifle pointing directly at the center of my forehead and met a set of eyes that caused my heart to race.

"Do you hear me, boy?!" the man wanted to confirm. His face was beet-red with anger.

"Yes, sir."

"Well, the law should be coming soon. I done called them. I'm going to hold this gun on you until they get here."

Within fifteen minutes a black and white police cruiser came to a sudden stop just in front of where I and the landlord stood. To juvenile hall once again I was transported.

"You didn't listen did you?" the young Henderson said shaking his head from side-to-side. "I told you that if you did not stop stealing you would wind up behind bars. Didn't I tell you that?"

"Yes, sir," I said in a low tone. My head lowered.

The young Henderson stood up from sitting down. He ran his hands across his head while he thought on the next thing to say. He inhaled and exhaled a heavy sigh before speaking again, "Man, I just don't know how to help you. Or is it you can't be helped?"

I brought my slumped shoulders up then down.

"You don't know?! Are you telling me that you don't know?!"

He waited for me to respond to that question. When I did not, he went on, "Man, you just got in trouble three months ago for beating that young dude down with a 380. You pistol-whipped him. You almost beat his brains out. What if you had killed him, Cedric? You want to be known as a murderer? Then you were sent back to juvenile hall. Aren't you tired of being locked up?"

"But he shouldn't have gone around the school telling everybody I was a Vice Lord when I'm a Disciple!"

The young Henderson stared at me in disbelief before speaking, "You gone try to justify that behavior, man?! Those are gangs! Listen to what you just said! Really, Cedric?! Really, man?!"

"Well, at least they treat me like family."

"What?! They treat you like family?! Is that what you said?!"

"Yes. In the gang I was the leader!"

"And look where your leadership got you! Wow, man!

From Persecution To Praise

What do you hate about being free?" I was sentenced to one and a half years in jail.

Cedric Doss

THE VOICE OF THE LORD

Out of jail with no place to go, I walked the streets of West Point, Mississippi in tattered, dirty clothes and an empty stomach.

"Get up and get out of here right now!" an unidentified white man shouted. "The post office is not where you stay! Get up and don't you ever come in here again with your nasty self! Go take a bath!"

Slowly, I sat up as my blurry, sleepy eyes fell on several unfamiliar faces opening and closing their mailboxes as they retrieved their mail. Most of them, those that looked down at me anyway, detested me. One-by-one, as they walked passed me lying on the floor of the post office they turned up their long noses in disgust. One red-faced man remained glaring down hard at me.

"Didn't I tell you to get your nasty ass up out of here?!" he started, lifting his foot to kick me. "I don't mean in a few minutes!" he went on. "I mean right now!"

I moved faster than I ever had getting out of the angry man's way. I got to my feet and went straight to the exit door. "Get!" the man called after me.

Outside old man winter had definitely sat in. The thin jacket that I had found in the garbage was not thick enough to keep the north wind from biting into my brown skin. I pulled a half-a-pint of whiskey from inside of my jacket, unscrewed the top, brought it to my waiting lips and took a big swig. I frowned, closed and opened my eyes. Heavy drinking had become my way of coping. Just as I swallowed hard the brown liquor I heard a voice, "I HAVE SOMETHING FOR YOU TO DO." I looked all around to see if I saw anyone there. There was no one.

"I HAVE SOMETHING FOR YOU TO DO.". It was the same voice again, repeating the same exact words as before. I continued to walk, picking up the pace, staring straight ahead as the wind beat against my already cold face.

"I HAVE A PLAN FOR YOUR LIFE." The voice added.

Thinking that I was going crazy, I brought both of my

cold hands and covered both my ears trying to drown out the voice that would not stop speaking to me.

"I HAVE SOMETHING FOR YOU TO DO."

Quickly, I hurried toward a port-a-john that was sitting on a construction site hoping that I could outpace the voice. I swung the door open. Immediately, the wind caught it and swung it wider hitting the side of the small building with a loud thud. Inside, the small area protected me from the wind. For the remainder of the day and night I rested there.

Hunger pains caused me to look for food the next day. It had been three whole days since I had a decent meal. My stomach growled like an angry bear was inside of it.

As I did most evenings, I began roaming the streets looking for food and a place to lay my weary soul for the night. "GO TO THE CHURCH", the voice spoke to me again. When I looked around my eyes fell on a large steeple rising up from the roof of the Presbyterian Church in downtown West Point. There was an elderly white lady getting into her car in the parking lot.

"Hey, ma'am!" I called out to her.

The lady stopped and looked in the direction of the strange, hungry, homeless, raggedy black man—me. "Yes," she started. "Can I help you?"

"Yes, ma'am. Please give me some money to get me something to eat. I'm so hungry." I asked.

The lady walked closer to me with her head turned sideways examining me. "You need more than some food. You need some clothes, too" she began. "You're not dressed for this cold weather. You ought to be freezing!"

"Yes, ma'am. I am, but I just want enough money to get me something to eat."

To my surprise the lady reached inside of her purse and pulled out a one hundred dollar bill and handed it to me. "Now go get you something to eat and buy you some clothes. The ones you have on are filthy."

Gladly and unbelievably, I took the one hundred dollar bill from the fingertips of the strange woman with wide eyes. I could not believe she had given me that much money.

"Better yet," she said to me closing the door shut to her vehicle and leading the way. "Come inside of the church."

Inside was a sea of unfamiliar faces who were all sitting down to a fellowship meal. I felt nervous and afraid. "Sit down right here," the lady ordered me. She left me sitting there and when she returned, she had something wrapped in shiny silver foil. "Now here is a plate of food. Come back when our pastor is here." I took the plate covered in shiny silver foil and turned to leave. "Wait a minute," the lady said coming after me. I turned to stop thinking she had changed her mind.

Instead the lady and her husband carried me to a local hotel after taking me to Wal-Mart to shop. I rode in the backseat peering through the side window as we sped down the highway. I felt so grateful inside. I had not felt that way in some time now. Finally, since leaving Bigmama's and Bigdaddy's I felt like someone genuinely cared about me. There was an instant gratification swelling inside.

When we arrived at the hotel the gracious couple paid for two nights. "Our pastor will contact you within these two days," the lady's husband said. "Now, eat your food, take a hot bath and get you some sleep."

"Thank you! Thank you!" I said starting to cry.

"Hey, my brother. It's what God's people do. Now get in there. Wait a minute. Let's pray."

The man reached out to take both his wife's hand and mine. The prayer ended with a hearty and united, "Amen!" We all hugged and the couple left me alone with my feelings, but in better shape than they had found me in.

In the shower, I closed my eyes and let the hot water spray my face from the shower head. It felt amazing to my dirty skin. I lathered my body completely with the bar of oatmeal-colored soap before going under the shower head again. I dried off, changed into my new navy blue pajama bottoms and top and laid back the covers on the bed. I had to get on my knees and thank God. It was a must. Once I thanked Him over and over again, I climbed between the sheets with a big smile on my face and dozed off. I was not sleep for very long when I heard the soft still voice again, "PREACH MY WORD".

Immediately, I sat up on my elbows in shock looking all around the dark room. My heart pounded as if it wanted to jump through my freshly-bathed skin. The sliver of light peeping under the closed bathroom door shined on the room. Again, I saw no one. I reached up and used the back of my hand to wipe the beads of perspiration sprinkled across my forehead. Slowly, with my eyes still wide opened, and my heart beating wildly, I laid my head back until the soft pillow caught it. I drifted back to sleep.

Two days later, as promised, the pastor and his lovely wife of the Presbyterian Church, Pastor Steve and Sharon

Davis knocked on the hotel door where I was staying.

Hearing the knock on the door, I got up from sitting down and peeped through the curtains. Parked right in front of his hotel room was a black Fleetwod Cadillac. I figured it was Pastor Davis and his wife. Quickly, I unlocked the door and pulled it open to two smiling faces with the clearest and brightest blue eyes I had ever seen on a man or a woman.

"Come in!" I gladly invited the couple with a big smile on my face.

The couple stepped inside of the hotel room and immediately introduced themselves.

"Hi, Brother Cedric. My name is Pastor Steven Davis and this is my lovely wife and helpmeet, Sharon."

"Nice to meet you," I said putting my hand into the Pastor's outstretched hand first then into his wife's.

"One of my members at the church told me about you and your situation. We just wanted to come to speak to you ourselves and to let you know that we are here for you."

"Thank you, sir," I said, feeling my trust in them building. The man went on.

"We came down to meet you, but also to pay three

more nights for you and take you to Wal-Mart to buy you more groceries, clothes and a phone so that I can get in touch with you and you can get in touch with me."

I could not believe what I was hearing. Here stood in front of me people who had no idea about who I was or had been. "They don't even know me." I thought to myself. I'm a thief. I'm a criminal. I beat a man nearly to death. I was given away as a child. I spent time in juvenile hall, not once, but twice. I spent one and a half years in jail. I have out-of-wedlock- children. I drink heavy. I have been homeless for more than a year. Me? Are you sure?

"Yes, I know what you're thinking and it doesn't matter to us what you have done. We are here to offer you another beginning. Do you want it?"

It did not take me a minute to think about it. I readily said, "Yes!"

"Great! Then come on let's get to Wal-Mart!"

I followed on the heels of Mrs. Davis while she followed on the heels of her husband. The couple climbed into the front seat while I climbed into the back seat. The smell of the black leather wafted through the air catching my nose. I inhaled then exhaled then mouthed, Thank you, Lord. I was beginning to feel like a real human.

From Persecution To Praise

The Davis' treated me like a member of their church. In fact, they treated me better—more like a son. Their goodness was shown in many ways beyond that day. Money, a trailer, gifts and that nice black Fleetwood Cadillac. Yes they gave all this to me even job referrals. The list went on and on. Members of the church also showed me love and gave me more yard work than I could handle.

I praised God! I praised him because I did not deserve this love and compassion he had placed in these people's heart towards me. They fed and clothed me. The allowed me to work which restored my faith in me. I could be a civilized person. It helped me work off the residue of my anger and hatred at my life and those that played a part in it. God had turned all of my persecution into a praise. It was a praise that could only give him glory.

God never relented. He continued to speak to me and calling me to do his will. I ran from it for several years, my call to preach. I gave into God's determination to do His will later. I had a powerful testimony, and I presented it at Siloam Baptist Church in West Point.

Later, I was invited by my Aunt Louise and Aunt Pearl to come worship at the Second Baptist Church, Prairie,

Cedric Doss

Mississippi where the Pastor John Smith welcomed me with opened arms and there I began the ministry that God had placed inside of me long before I was even born.

Prologue

Paul's belief rested on the basis that if the new doctrine was of God, no man could overthrow it, and if the new doctrine was of man, it would certainly perish on its own (Acts 5:34-39). Because Gamaliel was esteemed by many, his counsel was heeded, and God used his counsel to give the infant church a launching pad.

At the martyrdom of Stephen, where Paul played an official role, believers fled wherever they could. In their dispersion, Paul pursued them beyond the borders of Philistine and into Damascus. He carried with him a letter from the High Priest to the synagogues giving Paul authorization to arrest and bring to Jerusalem any person who had sought a place of refuge in the Syrian city. Since the compositions of the High Priest was highly regarded in the synagogues, his authority in matters of religion, was upheld by the Roman power. The persecution of Christians was no doubt repugnant to Paul's fine inner sensitivities, still, he thought what he was doing by persecuting the Christians was right. Lost. His fury against the Christians only increased as the Christians spread to foreign cities.

On his way to Damascus, Paul (then Saul) came face-to-face with the vision of the risen Christ. When the supernatural Being, established Himself as "Jesus whom thou persecutest", Paul immediately recognized the error of his way and completely and immediately surrendered. Found. For three days Paul was blind. They were agonizing days as he further dealt with the Lord.

There was a man named Ananias of Damascus whose ministry consummated Paul's conversion experience, unfolding his divine Godly commission, ultimately opening the door to Christian fellowship. Found!

When traveling to an unfamiliar place, most of us have had the unfortunate happening of finding ourselves lost. Being lost is not so uncommon. What is uncommon is the fact that when we are lost we do not ask for directions. As a man, I have discovered my species is less likely to stop

From Persecution To Praise

someone and ask how to get back on the right road. Hence, continuing to travel in the wrong direction. It seems that men feel somewhat emasculated when we find ourselves lost and needing help to find our way. Because we are men and we are seen as the head, the leader, the like Saul before he be-came Paul, I, too, believed everyone that entered my space represented a violation of trust.

Although Paul was destined by God to become one of the greatest leaders of all time, initially those who had heard of him trusted him very little. He had become known as a persecutor of Christians. That kind of reputation did not sit very well with those who were following the path of Judaism. He was the ringleader of the campaign to repress those who followed Stephen. Stephen was one of the seven appointed to look after the daily distribution to the poor in the early church (Acts 6:1-6). Once Stephen had been stoned to death, Paul began to undermine the entire structure that the followers of Judaism had suffered greatly to establish. Paul could not imagine the reconciliation of the old and new order. Resolving to rid the region and ultimately the world of the new order that Stephen, the disciples and Jesus were traveling by foot to create, Paul resolved completely in his mind to stamp out the revolutionary movement. He desired for the old to remain relevant. He was not in favor of what Jesus was teaching to become more valuable than what had already been taught.

Today, so many people have similar notions: They do not want change. Change seems to insult who they are and what they represent. So rather than change they decide to launch a campaign, as Paul did, against those who propose change, in an effort to keep doing things the same old way, never considering whether or not the new way of doing things is more efficient or even effective.

Like Paul was lost; so was I. Like Paul, many people think that they are doing the right thing for the right reason. When in actuality, like Paul, they are not. This type of thinking causes us to behave in a way that seems to be okay, but it is really a sign of being lost and it has not been recognized as being such.

Paul had great teaching. So being lost has nothing to do with how much an individual knows. One can have as many degrees as a thermostat and yet be lost. Because at the feet of Gamaliel was where Paul sat to receive his training. This Gamaliel was a Pharisee and a prominent doctor of the law. He had extensive training in the Old Testament principles. In fact, when the Sanhedrin, the very enraged Sanhedrin, looked to kill the Apostles for their increasingly impudent (bold) testimony of Christ, Gamaliel rose up in the council and encouraged discreet caution on giving help and not receiving it.

Of course, none of us can be lost and found at the same time. Still, it is up to each of us how long we want to be lost and not be willing to ask for help. In fact, only a foolish person would be willing to continue down the same road knowing that the road is off course and will certainly not lead to the destination in question. So at what point do we ask for help in order to get back on the right road heading in the right direction? Again, only the person who is lost can answer that question. My advice to us is to ask for help immediately. We do not want to act as if we are not lost because we are so proud or operating in our deceptive ego and emotions. Be-having that way only sets us back further and brings on frustration that will show up and spill over into our lives and the lives around us. Get the map out. Search the route. Retrace it if necessary. The One who clearly gave us the map to get to our destination has done thorough research the roads we need to take to get us to where we are trying to go without the frustration and disappointment that remaining lost is sure to bring us.

You no longer have to lie and act like. Speak up. Say you are lost and need help getting back on the right road so that you can enjoy your journey. Admitting we are lost is the key to finding our way back. If we never admit then we never get to the truth. Without the truth, we remain lost.

Paul was knocked off of his beast on his journey. He was blinded. He heard the voice of God clearly. Instinctively, at that moment he knew that continuing the path he was traveling would lead him to a place of great regret. Just like God has mapped out a plan for your life, for my life, he had mapped out Paul's life as well. And if He has to knock us too off of our beasts, He will, so that we can get on the path He laid for us so that His will, not ours, will be done. Do you re-ally want God to have to do that to you so that you will find your way back to Him? We are lost without Him. Admit it and find your way to Him if you do not know Him or find your way back to Him if you have a relationship with Him but have found yourself traveling in the wrong direction. It is as simple as getting out your map (Bible) and tracing the route that was designed for you and me!

Now that I have had the opportunity to look back over my life, separating from certain customs and ways can be beneficial to the human's proper growth. When people go through tests, their testimonies have more influence on those who may be going through something similar. Some folks we just have to leave behind and that is God's will. Does not matter who they are. Does not matter what relation they are to you. It could be your mother. It could be your father. It could be your brother, your sister. God sees our lives from the beginning to the end. He is Alpha and He is Omega. He knows exactly what He is doing even though it does not look like it to the human's finite mind. When God has a plan for your life, then whatever it takes to get you on that path for manifesting His will, He will do it.

Detours can be beneficial to the plan. Nothing is ever simple. Nothing is ever straightforward in the plan of God. His plan will always lead us to some valleys and to some low places. If everything was always straight and never crooked then we would never have to depend on Him. Sure I was young. Sure most of you who are reading this have a measure of empathy and compassion for what my sisters and brothers and I went through. But it made me who I am today. I am who I am because He loved me and caused my life to not be straight, but just a bit crooked. I

Cedric Doss

owe it to the detour.

Pastor Doss's Biography

Chosen by God to preach, teach, prophesy, sing, pray, and a host of others, through it all Pastor Doss gives God all the praise and glory. He wasn't born with a silver spoon in his mouth nor was his childhood one of much peace. It prepared him though for the road ahead and the path God wanted him to take. It was a road of great humility and illumination prepping his feet with the gospel of peace and restoration.

His purpose in writing *From Persecution to Praise* was to allow readers to see the hand of God in and over his life. There is a path to purpose. On this path is the chastisement of Jesus Christ that perfects the saints. It takes a lot to destroy generations of sins. Once you finish reading this you will see and know of the hand of God.

His life and testimony shows that from a little child God sets out to keep you on the path of righteousness by equipping you with his word. Through all this turmoil the first family he was given to was a family full of God's word. God's word is what kept him alive. The word spoken over your life will carry you a mighty long way.

Pastor Doss has compassion for the young men of today. They are living a life close or even worse than his. If you can speak a word over their life. Speak blessings and not curses. They will live and not die!

Though he's lived in several Mississippi towns, he gladly makes Prairie, Mississippi his home, and is the proud pastor of the Mt. Moriah M.B. Church. For preaching or speaking engagements or to host a book signing, please contact him at 662-319-1402.

From Persecution To Praise

From Persecution To Praise

Cedric Doss

From Persecution To Praise

Cedric Doss

www.ingramcontent.com/pod-product-compliance
Lightning Source LLC
Chambersburg PA
CBHW020649300426
44112CB00007B/301